Economics
For Commoners

ROBIN HAHNEL

Copyright © 2019 Robin Hahnel

All rights reserved.

ISBN: 9781092508735

CONTENTS

Preface ... iv
Introduction: Economics and Society ... 1

Part One: Positive Economics

1. Production ... 5
2. Prices, Wages, and Profits ... 8
3. Incorporating the Environment ... 12
4. Macroeconomics: Aggregate Demand as Leading Lady ... 14
5. Money, Banks, and Finance ... 24

Part Two: Normative Economics

6. Getting the Most from Our Work ... 37
7. Preserving the Natural Environment ... 44
8. Distributive Justice ... 49

Conclusion: What Lies Ahead? ... 70

PREFACE

This short book distills economic wisdom down to its most essential insights to make it accessible to anyone with a high school education who is willing to engage a line of reasoning. In a world where so many obfuscate, distort, and misrepresent economic argument for venal purposes, citizens are wise to arm themselves with basic *economic literacy* to avoid being cowed or misled. This short book provides a relatively painless immunization.

INTRODUCTION: ECONOMICS AND SOCIETY

Let's begin by making clear what economics is… and is not.

In order to survive every human society must produce and consume what has been referred to by some as "our daily bread" and by others as "the material means of subsistence." As we will soon discuss, people use various inputs from the natural environment – land, water, minerals, and environmental *sink* storage capacities – to produce and distribute a *surplus* of goods we need and/or desire. Economics studies how we go about doing this:

- How is this activity organized and managed?

- What are the predictable consequences when these activities are guided by particular economic institutions, such as markets and private enterprise?

- What are better and worse outcomes?

But before we proceed to answer these questions, we should remember that in order to survive all human societies must do other things as well.

- Societies must procreate, socialize, and educate new generations -- and people create *reproductive systems* which govern *gender relations* to do this.

- Societies must resolve conflicts among their own members -- and people establish *political systems* to do this.

- And finally, every society must mediate relations among historically distinct internal communities, and conduct relations with external communities as well – and people establish what we might call *community systems* to do this.

In short, the economic system is not the only important system in society. The reproductive, political, and community *spheres of social life* are just as necessary as the economic sphere.

1

Moreover, there is no reason to presume, *in theory*, that one sphere of social life is *necessarily* more important than any other. In any historical society -- with its particular political, economic, reproductive, and community systems -- one sphere may influence another sphere more than vis-a-versa. And in order to understand what makes this society "tick," so to speak, that would be an important "truth" to ascertain. But this is something which must be discovered by studying the dynamics of particular historical societies, not something that can be deduced from social theory alone.

So not only is the economy not the "be all and end all," the extent to which the economy influences other spheres of social life, and vis-a-versa, is something that must be discovered through empirical investigation.[1] Nonetheless, there is no doubt that the economic sphere of social life is very important in most societies today -- both in its own right, and because of how it constrains and shapes our political, reproductive, and community life as well.

A final note, before beginning: This book does not evaluate the pros and cons of many important economic policies such as a minimum wage, single-payer healthcare, rent control, tax reform, carbon cap and trade programs, etc. Instead it provides readers with *economic literacy* – a basic understanding of how our economy works and how to evaluate its performance – which is necessary for readers to sensibly engage debates about these and other policies.

---

[1] For a more extensive discussion of economics and social theory see chapter 1 in Robin Hahnel, *The ABCs of Political Economy: A Modern Approach*, 2nd edition. (London UK: Pluto Press, 2014).

PART ONE: POSITIVE ECONOMICS

Sometimes economists simply try to explain how the economy works. This is often referred to as *positive economics*. The first five chapters concentrate on different aspects of that task:

1. How can we conceptualize and analyze what goes on in production?

2. In a capitalist economy -- i.e. an economy where production is carried out in privately owned enterprises in pursuit of profits, and goods and services are bought and sold in markets -- how are prices, wages, and profits determined?

3. How does the natural environment factor in?

4. In capitalist economies, what causes large scale unemployment and inflation?

5. What do money, banks, and finance have to do with any of this?

1 PRODUCTION

People use various inputs from the natural environment to produce a *surplus* of goods we need or desire. But it is useful to describe production in more detail. In any year there are certain known *feasible technologies* for how to turn a list of *inputs* of different kinds into a list of *outputs* of different kinds.

Primary inputs are inputs that are not outputs of any economic production process. They are either inputs provided by the natural environment, such as iron ore, water in aquifers, top soil, and sink capacities for storing wastes like carbon emissions. Or they are labor services of different kinds, such as carpentry, welding, computer programming, and nursing. *Produced inputs* are outputs of other production processes, such as steel, cloth, and lathes. If they are used up entirely during the year in which they are produced they are called *intermediate goods*. If they last and can be used for more than one year they are called *capital goods*.

Outputs can be *final goods* for consumption, such as pasta and T-shirts, intermediate or capital goods for production, or *wastes* such as particulate matter and carbon emissions released back into sinks in the natural environment. It is sometimes helpful to think of technologies as recipes, and all of the feasible technologies as the book of known recipes for how to turn a list of inputs into a list of outputs.

In modern economies the vast majority of inputs for any production process are produced as outputs of other production processes. As the economist Pierro Sraffa put it in the title of his only book, we mostly have "production of commodities by means of commodities." In which case it is useful to distinguish between the *gross* and *net* amount of any good produced during a year. Ignoring any detrimental effects on the environment for the moment, clearly what humans gain from whatever unpleasantness we experience when applying our labor during a year, is the *net output* produced, i.e. the amount of each produced good left over after subtracting the amount of that good which was used up producing itself and other goods during the year. Again, ignoring for the moment primary inputs from the natural environment and wastes released back into the environment, we can "model" production as follows:

Let $a(ij)$ represent the number of units of good i required to produce one unit of good j. And let L(j) be the number of hours of "direct" labor required to produce one unit of good j. In a two good economy we might have the following "recipes" for making each good:

a(11) = 0.3   a(12) = 0.2
a(21) = 0.2   a(22) = 0.4
L(1) = 1.0   L(2) = 0.5

The first column is the "recipe" used to make good 1. It takes workers in the industry producing the first good 1 hour working with 0.3 units of good 1 itself and 0.2 units of good 2 to produce 1 unit of good 1. It can help to think of the 1 hour of "direct labor" as the "stirring time" to transform the "ingredients," 0.3 units of good 1 and 0.2 units of good 2, into 1 unit of good 1. The second column is the "recipe" for making good 2. It takes workers in the second industry 0.5 hours working with 0.2 units of good 1 and 0.4 units of good 2 itself to produce 1 unit of good 2.

Notice we are assuming here that there is only one *primary*, i.e. non-produced, input in production, labor. Which means that for now we are assuming that everything is ultimately made by labor and labor alone. Yes, to make good 1 we need some of good 1 itself and some of good 2 along with labor – that is what the recipe for making good 1 says. But these inputs of goods 1 and 2 were, in turn, produced by labor.

Later we consider what happens when some other non-produced input from "nature" is required to produce things along with labor. But for now, we assume labor is the only non-produced input in our economy. Moreover, we also assume labor is *homogeneous*, i.e. there are not different kinds of labor -- carpenters, and welders, for example – where production sometimes requires one kind of labor and not the other. Again, we will discuss what happens if we relax this assumption later. And finally, for now we have only one recipe available for producing each good. Later when we discuss technological change we consider what will happen when there is more than one recipe for making each good.

The Economic Surplus

Given these technologies, what will happen if we apply 1 hour of labor producing good 1 and .5 hours of labor producing good 2?

$a(11) = 0.3 \quad a(12) = 0.2$
$a(21) = 0.2 \quad a(22) = 0.4$
$L(1) = 1.0 \quad L(2) = 0.5$

According to our recipes the 1 hour of labor working in the first industry will need .3 units of good 1 and .2 units of good 2 to work with, or stir. And the .5 hours of labor working in industry 2 will need .2 units of good 1 and .4 units of good 2 to work with. In which case what our recipes tell us is that we will get 1 unit of good 1 and 1 unit of good 2 as output. But we will have used up .3 units of good 1 plus .2 units of good 1 = .5 units of good 1(summing across the first row) to do so. And we will have used up .2 units of good 2 plus .4 units of good 2 = .6 units of good 2 (summing across the second row). So while we will have produced 1 unit of each good, we will have only produced 1 - .5 = .5 units of good 1 above and beyond what we used up. And we will have produced 1 - .6 = .4 units of good 2 above and beyond what we used up. In other words, what we will have gained from working 1 hour in industry 1 and .5 hours in industry 2 is a *surplus* of .5 units of good 1 and .4 units of good 2.

This is often described as the difference between *gross output* – in our case 1 unit of each good – and *net output* – in our case .5 units of good 1 and .4 units of good 2. Notice that if, when we sum across each row, we got 1.0, i.e. we do not have a positive net output of either good, this would mean that our known technologies were not productive – they were not capable of producing any surplus at all no matter how many hours we worked with them. But as long as when we sum across both rows we never exceed 1, and for at least one row the result is less than 1 -- and therefore we have a positive surplus of at least one good – we say *the economy is productive, i.e. capable of producing a physical surplus.*[2]

---

[2] For different ways to define what it means for a multi-good economy to produce an economic surplus see section A.2 in Appendix A of Robin Hahnel, *Income Distribution and Environmental Sustainability* (New York: Routledge, 2017).

2 PRICES, WAGES, AND PROFITS

Now that we have a convenient way to model production, and know what it means to say that feasible technologies are productive, i.e. the economy is capable of producing a physical surplus, what will happen if this *productive economy* is run as a capitalist economy where some people, capitalists, hire others, workers, to be their employees?

Let $p(1)$ be the price of a unit of good 1, $p(2)$ be the price of a unit of good 2, w be the hourly wage rate, and $r(1)$ and $r(2)$ be the rates of profit received by capitalists in industry 1 and 2 respectively. The first step is to write down an equation for each industry that expresses the truism that revenue minus cost for the industry is, by definition, equal to industry profit. If we divide both sides of this equation by the number of units of output the industry produces we get the truism that revenue per unit of output minus cost per unit of output must equal profit per unit of output. Another way of saying this is: *cost per unit of output plus profit per unit of output must equal revenue per unit of output*. This is the equation we want to write for each industry.

The second step is to write down what cost per unit of output and revenue per unit of output will be for each industry. For industry 1 it takes $a(11)$ units of good 1 itself to make a unit of output of good 1. That will cost $p(1)a(11)$. It also takes $a(21)$ units of good 2 to make a unit of output of good 1. That will cost $p(2)a(21)$. So $[p(1)a(11) + p(2)a(21)]$ are the non-labor costs of making one unit of good 1. Since it takes $L(1)$ hours of labor to make a unit of good 1 and the wage per hour is w, the labor cost of making a unit of good 1 is $wL(1)$. Revenue per unit of output of good 1 is simply $p(1)$ times 1 unit of output, or $p(1)$.

What is profit per unit of output in industry 1? By definition profits are revenues minus costs, so profits per unit of output must be equal to revenues per unit of output minus cost per unit of output. Also by definition the rate of profit is profits divided by whatever part of costs a capitalist must pay for in advance. Dividing both the numerator and denominator by the number of units of output in industry 1 gives us the truism that the rate of profit in industry 1 is equal to the profit per unit of output in industry 1 divided by whatever part of costs per unit of output capitalists must advance in industry 1. Therefore, the *profit per unit of output in industry 1 must be equal to the rate of profit for industry 1 times the cost per unit of output capitalists must advance in industry 1.*

Assume that capitalists must pay for all costs in advance. So the cost per unit of output capitalists must advance in industry 1 is [p(1)a(11) + p(2)a(21) + wL(1)]. Also assume that the rate of profit capitalists receive is the same in both industries, r, since otherwise capitalists would move from industries with a lower rate of profit to industries with a higher rate of profit until their profit rates became the same. Therefore:

profit per unit of output in industry 1 = r[p(1)a(11) + p(2)a(21) + wL(1)]

Finally, we are ready to write the accounting identity, or truism, that cost per unit of output plus profit per unit of output equals revenue per unit of output in the first industry:

[p(1)a(11) + p(2)a(21) + wL(1)] + r[p(1)a(11) + p(2)a(21) + wL(1)] = p(1)

Which can be rewritten as: (1+r) [p(1)a(11) + p(2)a(21) + wL(1)] = p(1). Writing a similar equation for industry 2 we get what are called the *price equations* for the economy:

(1) (1+r) [p(1)a(11) + p(2)a(21) + wL(1)] = p(1)
(2) (1+r) [p(1)a(12) + p(2)a(22) + wL(2)] = p(2)

In these price equations recall that a(11), a(21), a(12), a(22), L(1), and L(2) are all technological *givens*. Which means that we have 2 equations with 4 *unknowns*: two *distributive variables*, w and r, and two prices, p(1) and p(2). However, we are only interested in *relative* prices, i.e. how many units of one good trade for how many units of another good. If we set the price of good 2 equal to 1, p(2) = 1, then p(1) tells us how many units of good 2 one unit of good 1 exchanges for, and w tells us how many units of good 2 a worker can by with her hourly wage. The rate of profit, r, is a pure number such as .05, which would represent a 5% rate of profit, or "return" on the financial value of the capitalist's outlay. So we now have 2 equations in 3 unknowns: w, the *real* hourly wage rate, r, the uniform rate of profit for capitalists in both industries in the economy, and p(1), the price of good 1 *relative* to the price of good 2. Unfortunately we do not have as many equations as unknowns, and therefore cannot yet solve for the values of our unknown variables. However, we can ask: What would r and p(1) in this economy be if the wage rate were, for example, w=.690909? In which case we simply substitute w=.690909 and p(2)=1, along with the data representing our technologies (or recipes) for producing the two goods, into the two price equations and solve for p(1) and r. Solving:

$(1+ r)[.3p(1) + .2(1) + 1(.690909)] = p(1)$
$(1+ r)[.2p(1) + .4(1) + .5(.690909)] = 1$

Gives: p(1) = 1.27273 and r = .00000 or r = 0.000%.[3]

And we can ask: What if the conditions of *class struggle* are such that workers' wage is only .500000 units of good 2 per hour? What will p(1) and r be? Solving:

$(1 + r)[.3p(1) + .2(1) + 1(.500000)] = p(1)$
$(1 + r)[.2p(1) + .4(1) + .5(.500000)] = 1$

Gives: p(1) = 1.19034 and r = .12604 or 12.604%.

And we can ask: What if the conditions of class struggle are such that workers only receive w = .400, what will p(1) and r be? Solving:

$(1 + r)[.3p(1) + .2(1) + 1(.400000)] = p(1)$
$(1 + r)[.2p(1) + .4(1) + .5(.400000)] = 1$

Gives: p(1) = 1.13746 and r = .20847 or 20.847%

In our example, as the wage rate falls from .690909 to .500000 to .400000 units of good 2 per hour, the rate of profit in the economy, r, rises from 0.000% to 12.604% to 20.847%. It is possible to prove that this negative relationship always holds: The wage and profit rates in this simple model of

---

[3] I used https://www.wolframalpha.com to solve all systems of two equations in two unknowns in this book, and readers can do likewise if they wish. Place the point finger on the red dot with positive values for both variables where the two curves cross in the graphical solution.

the economy are necessarily negatively, or "inversely" related.[4] The most important conclusion from this analysis is that, not surprisingly, there seems to be a conflict of interest between those who work for others for a wage and those who employ them over how to distribute output between them.

Less important, but also worth noting, is that as we change from one possible combination of wage and profit rate in the economy to another – from (w = .690909, r = .00000) to (w = .500000, r = .12604) to (w = .400000, r = .20847) -- the price of good 1 relative to good 2, p(1), changes from 1.27273 to 1.19034 to 1.13746 *even though production technologies are the same in all three situations*. Clearly, a second important "economic fact of life" is that relative prices are not determined by technology alone. Income distribution also plays a role in price determination.

---

[4] See theorem 13 in *Income Distribution and Environmental Sustainability*.

3 INCORPORTING THE ENVIRONMENT

Before going any further we need to add the natural environment to our simple model. We need to take into account the fact that in addition to produced inputs and labor, production requires *primary inputs* from the natural environment. We can do this by including them as inputs into our recipes as follows. Suppose 0.3 units of "nature" must be present to produce a unit of good 1, and 0.2 units of "nature" must be present to produce 1 unit of good 2. Further, suppose that u is the rent per unit of nature which must be paid to its owner, and capitalists must pay for all inputs – produced inputs, labor, and nature – in advance. Now our recipes look like this:

a(11) = 0.3   a(12) = 0.2
a(21) = 0.2   a(22) = 0.4
L(1) = 1.0   L(2) = 0.5
N(1) = 0.3   N(2) = 0.2

And our price equations look like this:

(3) (1+r)[p(1)a(11)+p(2)a(21)+wL(1)+uN(1)] = p(1)
(4) (1+r)[p(1)a(12)+p(2)a(22)+wL(2)+uN(2)] = p(2)

Substituting in our numerical values for the coefficients and setting p(2) equal to 1 we have:

(1+r)[.3p(1) + .2 + 1.0w + .3u)] = p(1)
(1+r)[.2p(1) + .4 + .5w + .2u] = 1

The four unknowns we need to solve for are p(1), w, r, and u. If we set two of the distributive variables equal to zero, we can solve for p(1) and the maximum possible value of the other distributive variable. Doing this we find:

w(max) = .690909 and p(1) = 1.27273 when r = u = 0
r(max) = .798059 and p(1) = .780776 when w = u = 0
u(max) = 1.90000 and p(1) = 1.10000 when w = r = 0

We can also discover what the effect of increasing the value of any distributive variable is on the other distributive variables. Suppose, for example, instead of setting w = u = 0 we increase w to .100, keep u = 0 and solve for r. We find that r falls from its maximum value, .798059, when both of the other distributive variables are zero, to .58435. Or, if we raise r from zero to .10000 and keep w = 0 we discover that u falls from its maximum of 1.900 to 1.48545.[5]

It can be proved that in this model there is a negative relationship between all three distributive variables – the wage rate, the profit rate, and rent per unit of "nature" required -- just as there was in the system with only the two distributive variables, w and r. In other words, there is an inherent conflict of interest between those who receive their income as wages, those who receive their income as profits or dividends, and those who receive their income as rent. Moreover, this negative relationship holds even when we expand the system to account for multiple different "primary" inputs from nature, such as iron ore, petroleum, and water from aquifers, in addition to land of different qualities, each with its own rental rate, as well as multiple different kinds of labor, such as welding, carpentry, and computer programming labor, each with its own wage rate.[6]

---

[5] As before, all these solutions can be found using https://www.wolframalpha.com.

[6] See theorem 19 in *Income Distribution and Environmental Sustainability*.

4 MACROECONOMICS: AGGREGRATE DEMAND AS LEADING LADY

In the midst of the Great Depression John Maynard Keynes created what came to be known as *macroeconomic theory* to explain the causes and remedies for large scale unemployment and inflation -- which prior economic theory shed little light on. What we might call the "leading lady" in Keynes' new drama was *aggregate demand,* the demand for all final goods and services in general. By focusing on aggregate demand Keynes was able to explain why the production of goods and services can fall, even though technologies are no less productive, and the supplies of labor, resources, and capital goods are just as plentiful as before. Keynes explained why these economic "downturns" – *recessions* when mild, and *depressions* when large -- can occur and become self-reinforcing. Most importantly Keynes also explained how government fiscal and monetary policies could be used to combat unemployment or inflation when these problems occur.

The Macro Law of Supply and Demand

The key to Keynes' revolutionary new thinking is something we might call the *macro law of supply and demand* which says: *aggregate supply will follow aggregate demand if it can.* Aggregate supply is simply the supply of all final goods and services produced as a whole, or in the aggregate, which economists call gross domestic product, or GDP. Aggregate demand is the demand for all final goods and services as a whole. It includes the demand from all the *households* in the economy for shirts, shoes, toys, etc., the demand from all *businesses* in the economy for drill presses, conveyor belts, cranes, etc., and the demand from every level of *government* for missiles, highways, park playground equipment, etc.

The rationale behind the macro law of supply and demand is as follows: The business sector is not clairvoyant and cannot know in advance what demand will be for their products. Of course individual businesses spend considerable time, energy, and money trying to estimate, and through advertising influence what the demand for their particular good or service will be. But in the end businesses produce what amounts to their best guess of what they will be able to sell, and the business sector as a whole produces as much as they think they will be able to sell at prices they find acceptable. They don't produce more because they wouldn't want to produce goods and services they don't expect to be able to sell. And they don't produce less because this would mean foregoing profitable opportunities.

What if the business community is overly optimistic? That is, what will happen if the business sector produces more than it turns out they are able to sell? In this case most businesses will find they are selling less from their inventories than they are producing, and therefore they are adding to inventory stocks each month. If inventories continue to pile up in warehouses businesses will eventually cut back on production rates. When this occurs the supply of goods and services in the aggregate will fall to meet the lower level of aggregate demand – *i.e. aggregate supply will follow aggregate demand* **down**.

What if businesses are overly pessimistic? That is, what will happen if the business sector produces less than it turns out they are able to sell? They will discover their error soon enough because sales rates will be higher than production rates, and inventory stocks in warehouses will be depleted. So even if they initially underestimate the demand for their products, businesses will increase production when they discover their error, and therefore production, or aggregate supply, will rise to meet aggregate demand – *i.e. aggregate supply will follow aggregate demand* **up**.

However, there might be circumstances in which the business sector won't be able to increase production even when they want to. What if all the productive resources in the economy are already fully and efficiently employed? In this case the increase in labor and resources necessary for one business to increase its production would have to come from some other business where they are already employed, so the increased production of one business would be matched by a decrease in the production of some other business, and production as a whole, or aggregate supply could not increase. This is why the macro law of supply and demand says that *aggregate supply will follow aggregate demand* **if it can**. If the economy is already producing the most it can, if it is already producing what economists call full employment or potential gross domestic product, potential GDP, aggregate supply will not be able to follow aggregate demand should the aggregate demand for goods and services exceed potential GDP.

This simple, common sense "law" provides powerful insights about what level of production an economy will settle on, and whether or not the labor, resources, and productive capacities of the economy will or will not be fully utilized. Keynes emphasized that the answer to the question: "How much will we produce?" is not necessarily: "As much as we can, i.e. potential GDP." If the demand for goods and services in the aggregate is equal to potential GDP, then when aggregate supply follows aggregate demand we will indeed produce up to our capabilities. But if aggregate demand is less than potential GDP, then, when aggregate supply follows aggregate demand, production will be less than the amount we are capable of producing, and consequently, there will be unemployed labor and idle productive capacity. This does not happen because the business community wants to produce less than it can. It happens because it is not in their interest to produce more than they can sell.

Any changes in the size or skills of the labor force, quantity or quality of productive resources, size or quality of the capital stock, or state of productive knowledge will change the amount of goods and services we *can* produce, i.e. the level of potential GDP. But what will determine the amount we *will* produce is the level of aggregate demand, and only changes in aggregate demand will lead to changes in what we *do* produce.

To summarize: According to the macro law of supply and demand if aggregate demand is equal to potential GDP, actual GDP will become equal to potential GDP. But if aggregate demand is less than potential GDP, actual GDP will be equal to the level of aggregate demand and less than potential GDP.

But what will happen if aggregate demand is greater than potential GDP? In this case businesses will try to increase production levels to take advantage of favorable sales opportunities. But once the economy has reached potential GDP, as much as businesses might want to increase production further, as a whole they won't be able to. Instead, frustrated employers will try to outbid one another for employees and resources -- pulling up wages and resource prices. And frustrated consumers will try to outbid one another for fewer final goods and services than there is demand for, pulling up prices of final goods in what we call *demand pull inflation* -- a rise in the general level of prices caused by demand for goods and services in excess of the maximum level of production we are capable of.

Aggregate demand, AD, is composed of the consumption demand of all the households in the economy -- what economists call *private consumption*, C; the demand for investment, or capital goods by all businesses in the economy -- what economists call *investment demand*, I; and the demand for public goods and services by local, state, and the federal government – *government spending*, G. In other words, AD = C + I + G.

One of Keynes' greatest insights was that even though businesses would try to adjust to discrepancies between aggregate demand and supply when they arose, that in addition to the *equilibrating* forces described in the macro law of supply and demand, *dis-equilibrating* forces could operate in the economy as well. In particular, Keynes pointed out that weak demand for goods and services leading to layoffs and downward pressure on wages was likely to further weaken aggregate demand by reducing the buying power of the majority of consumers and therefore private consumption demand. Which, he argued, would in turn lead to more layoffs and downward pressure on wages, which would reduce the demand for goods even further. The logical result was a downward spiral in which aggregate demand, and therefore production, moved farther and farther away from potential GDP. Keynes ridiculed his contemporaries' faith that excess supply of labor during the Great Depression would prove self-eliminating as wages fell. He quipped that no matter how cheap employees became, employers were not likely to hire workers when they had no reason to believe they could sell the goods those workers would make.

In sum, Keynes pointed out that the demand reducing effect of falling wages on employment might well outweigh the cost reducing effect of lower labor costs on employment -- particularly during a recession when finding buyers, not lowering production costs, is the chief concern of businesses. As a result Keynes distained the complacency of his colleagues in face of high and rising levels of unemployment during the Great Depression based on what he considered to be their unwarranted faith that (1) demand *should* be sufficient to buy full employment levels of output, and (2) unemployment *should* be eliminated by falling wages which make labor cheaper.

To arrest this downward spiral Keynes preached that the government should increase aggregate demand directly by increasing its own demand for public goods and services, G, and/or induce an increase in consumer demand by reducing personal income taxes, T, and/or induce an increase in investment

demand by decreasing business taxes. Since these measures will increase the government budget deficit, T - G, it is often criticized as fiscally irresponsible. Keynes and his followers reply that what is irresponsible is to allow the economy to sink deeper and remain in recession or depression when a little *pump priming* – increasing G and/or decreasing T -- can increase employment, output, and income – and when income rises increase tax revenues and thereby eliminate budget deficits as well.

As explained, aggregate demand, AD, is the sum of household consumption demand, C, business investment demand, I, and government spending, G. Keynes pointed out that household consumption demand will depend positively on household income and negatively on personal taxes. Business investment will be determined by a host of factors that affect how optimistic businesses are about future business conditions, the cost of borrowing to finance new investment projects, and business taxes. And the federal government can decide to spend whatever it wants independent of how much taxes it decides to collect, since the government can always run a *budget surplus*, collecting more taxes than it spends, and can always finance a *budget deficit* by selling treasury bonds to spend more than it collects in taxes.

But before we can turn all this Keynesian wisdom into a macroeconomic model to explore how fiscal and monetary policy can be used to combat recessions and inflation, one task remains: How much income will consumers have? We have to know their level of income before we can determine how high their consumption demand will be. The answer is given by a simple truism I call the *pie principle* which says: *the size of the pie we can eat is always equal to the size of the pie we baked.* This truism is easiest to see if we pretend for a moment the economy only produces one kind of good. Suppose we produce only shmoos -- which we eat, wear, live in, and use (like machines) to produce more shmoos. If a shmoo factory produces 100 shmoos what can happen to them? Some will be used to pay the workers' wages. However many are left over will belong to the factory owners as profits. How much did our shmoo factory contribute to gross domestic product? 100 shmoos. How much income was generated and distributed at the same time by our shmoo factory? 100 shmoos -- no matter how that income was divided between wages and profits. Suppose the workers were powerful and succeeded in getting paid 95 shmoos in wages. Then profits would be 100 - 95 = 5 shmoos. And wages, 95 shmoos, plus profits, 5 shmoos, add up to 95 + 5 = 100 shmoos of total income. On the other hand, suppose employers were powerful and only paid out 60 shmoos in wages. Then employers' profits would be 100 - 60 = 40 shmoos. And wages, 60 shmoos, plus profits, 40 shmoos, add up to 60 + 40 = 100 shmoos of total income again. The sum of the workers' wages and owners' profits cannot exceed 100 shmoos, nor can it be less than 100 shmoos. Since the same will hold for every shmoo factory, gross domestic product, measured in shmoos, and gross domestic income, measured in shmoos, have to be the same in an economy producing one good.

This conclusion extends to an economy that produces many different goods and services where we use some kind of money, like the dollar, to measure both the value of all the goods and services produced and the value of all the income generated and distributed in the process. The level of income in the economy will always be equal to the value of goods and services produced in the economy because the size of the pie we can eat is always equal to the size of the pie we baked. Which is why we don't need two different symbols for gross domestic product, or output, GDP, and gross domestic income, GDI, in our model and the equations below. We can use the letter Y to stand for the value of all final goods and services produced, GDP, *and* for the value of all income paid out, GDI, since they always have the same value.

The Simple Keynesian Macroeconomic Model

We can embody all this logic into a simple Keynesian macroeconomic model of an economy as follows:

$Y = C + I + G$. On the left side of the equation Y represents GDP, or aggregate supply, AS. On the right side of the equation (C+I+G) represents aggregate demand, AD. As explained, we rely on the macro law of supply and demand to bring AS into equality with AD, and call this equation our *macroeconomic equilibrium condition*.

$C = a + MPC(Y-T)$. C is aggregate private consumption. Y is household income, or GDI, but because the pie principle assures us that GDI must be the same as GDP, we can use the same letter, Y, to represent both GDP and GDI. T is personal income taxes, and therefore (Y-T) is consumers' *disposable income*. "a" represents *autonomous consumption*, the amount households spend independent of their disposable income. MPC is called the *Marginal Propensity to Consume* (rather than save) out of disposable income, and must be a fraction between zero and one. Investment demand, I, will be whatever it happens to be, I*. And the government will decide how much it wants to spend, G*, and tax, T*.

We define *equilibrium GDP, or Y(e), to be the level of production at which aggregate supply* **would** *be equal to aggregate demand*. Depending on how great aggregate demand is, it may be possible for the business sector to produce equilibrium GDP or it may not. If AD is less than or equal to potential GDP, which is traditionally called Y(f) for "full employment GDP," it is possible for the economy to produce Y(e), and the macro law predicts that actual GDP will eventually become equal to Y(e). But if AD is greater than potential GDP actual production cannot equal Y(e), but must stop short at Y(f). However, we can still ask: How high *would* GDP have to be in order for aggregate supply to equal aggregate demand? And the answer, Y(e), has significance because when the business sector produces all it can, Y(f), Y(e) - Y(f) will be the amount of excess demand for final goods and services in the economy giving us a measure of how much demand pull inflation to expect. For any given I*, G*, and T* we can use the model to find the equilibrium level of GDP. All we have to do is substitute into the equilibrium condition, and note that the Y that satisfies this condition is equilibrium GDP, Y(e):

(5) Y(e) = a + MPC[Y(e) - T*] + I* + G*

If we know MPC, a, I*, T* and G* we can solve this equation for Y(e). After "solving" for Y(e) we can compare it with potential GDP, Y(f), to see if we will have an unemployment problem, an inflation problem, or neither. If Y(f) - Y(e) is positive, we have an *unemployment gap* in the economy of that many billions of dollars because the economy will only produce Y(e). The size of the unemployment gap represents the value of the goods and services that we could have produce but did not produce because there wasn't sufficient demand for goods and services to warrant hiring all of the labor force, and using all the available resources and productive capacity the economy has. Another way of interpreting the size of an unemployment gap is as the value of the goods and services that those unemployed workers and resources could have produced but didn't because they were unemployed. If Y(f) - Y(e) is negative, we have an *inflation gap* in the economy because the level of aggregate demand which is equal to Y(e) is that many billions of dollars greater than the maximum value of goods and services the economy is presently capable of producing, Y(f).

For example, suppose a = 90, MPC = 3/4, I* = 100, T* = 40, G* = 40. Substituting these values in to our equilibrium condition we have:

Y(e) = 90 +(3/4)(Y(e) – 40) + 100 + 40

Which can be solved to find that Y(e) = 800,[7] meaning that the business sector will eventually produce 800 billion dollars' worth of goods and services. However, what if Y(f) = 900, i.e. the economy is capable of producing 900 billion dollars' worth of goods and services? In this case the economy will fall short of baking as big a pie as we could have by 100 billion dollars. We will have unemployed labor and resources that *would* have produced an additional 100 billion *had* they been employed -- but they won't because aggregate demand is only 800 billion so that's all the business sector can sell. For what it's worth, in this example the government budget is balanced (T* - G* = 40 - 40 = 0), but the economy is in a recession, only producing 800/900 = .89, or 89% of all it could.

Fiscal Policy

We are now ready to understand the logic of *fiscal policy* defined as any changes in government spending and/or taxes. The microeconomic perspective on fiscal policy is that because individuals will not buy goods if they only enjoy a tiny fraction of the benefits they provide, the government must step in and provide *public goods* like parks and MX missiles. In this light the government should buy an amount of each public good up to the point where the additional benefit to all consumers collectively is equal to the additional cost to society of producing more of each public good. Then the government should simply collect enough taxes to pay for the public goods the government buys and makes available to the citizenry. In contrast, the macroeconomic perspective focuses on the fact that government spending and taxation affect aggregate demand as we have just seen, and therefore, by changing spending or taxes the government can change the level of aggregate demand in the economy to eliminate an unemployment or inflation gap.

---

[7] As before, if you do not want to go through the algebraic manipulations necessary to solve this single equation in a single unknown, you can use https://www.wolframalpha.com to do it for you.

If the economy is suffering from an unemployment gap -- if there are people willing and able to work who can't find jobs, and productive capacity is sitting idle, so we are producing and consuming less than we could – by increasing G* the government could increase aggregate demand and thereby reduce the unemployment gap. Or, by reducing spending the government could decrease aggregate demand and reduce the size of any inflation gap in the economy. Changing taxes will also have a predictable effect on aggregate demand. If the government increases taxes disposable income will fall and household consumption demand will fall, which would be helpful if the economy is suffering from demand pull inflation. If the economy has an unemployment gap, reducing taxes would be helpful because it would increase households' disposable income, and induce them to consume more and thereby raise aggregate demand and equilibrium GDP.

For example, to eliminate the 100 billion dollar unemployment gap in our above example we simply substitute in what we want $Y(e)$ to be, which is $Y(f)$, into the equilibrium condition and solve for the level of government spending that would yield this result: Solving $900 = 90+3/4(900 - 40) + 100 + G'$ gives $G' = 65$. Since G* is initially 40, this means the government can eliminate the 100 billion dollar unemployment gap by increasing its spending by 25 billion dollars, from 40 to 65 billion. Or, alternatively we can calculate how much the government would have to reduce personal income taxes to eliminate the same unemployment gap: Solving $900 = 90+3/4(900 - T') + 100 + 40$ gives $T' = 6.67$. Since T* is initially 40, this means the government can also eliminate the unemployment gap by reducing taxes by 33.33 billion dollars.

In either case -- eliminating the unemployment gap to improve economic performance by increasing G or decreasing T -- requires running a budget deficit for the time being. But contrary to a great deal of popular opinion these days, this is always possible and generally well worthwhile. Any household or business which persists in spending more than its income will eventually run out of anyone willing to keep lending them money, and therefore go bankrupt. However, if the federal government ran out of customers for its treasury bonds – which is how the government borrows -- it could simply print more money to cover its deficit. Those who insist on applying reasoning appropriate for households and businesses -- or city and state governments for that matter -- to the federal government ignore this very important difference: It is legal, not counterfeiting, when the *federal* government prints more money! In any case, after the economy is back to performing up to its capacities, the budget can be rebalanced through increases in tax revenues that rising incomes automatically generate, and/or through reductions in spending once there is no longer need for further fiscal stimulus.

5 MONEY, BANKS, AND FINANCE

> A bank is a place where they lend you an umbrella in fair weather and ask for it back when it begins to rain. -- Robert Frost

We have learned a great deal about how the economy works already, but have not said a word about things that people normally assume economics is all about – money, banks, and finance. There is an important lesson here. What matters is what we produce, how it is distributed, and how all this affects the natural environment. That is, what is sometimes called the *real economy* is what actually matters. Money, banks, finance, and stock markets are only of peripheral interest. They are only important because they can affect these other things we care about.

We will discover in this chapter how money, banks, and finance work, and how they can sometimes improve, but sometimes diminish economic performance in the real economy. It is ironic that money and banks top the list of economic subjects that most baffle students, because money is just a clever invention to save time, and bankers, contrary to their stodgy reputations, substitute bigamy for proper marriages between borrowers and lenders -- with predictably disastrous consequences when both "wives" press their legal claims against their bank "husband" who has married them both.

Money: A Problematic Convenience

It is possible to have exchange, or market economies without money. A *barter economy* is one in which people exchange one kind of good directly for another kind of good. For instance, I grow potatoes because my land is best suited to that crop. My neighbor grows carrots because her land is better for carrots. But if we both like our stew with potatoes *and* carrots, we can accomplish this through barter exchange. On Saturday I take some of my potatoes to town, she takes some of her carrots, and we exchange a certain number of pounds of potatoes for a certain number of pounds of carrots. No money is involved as goods are exchanged directly for other goods.

Notice that in barter exchange the act of supplying is inextricably linked to an equivalent and act of demanding. I cannot supply potatoes in the farmer's market without simultaneously demanding carrots. And my neighbor cannot supply carrots without simultaneously demanding potatoes. Having learned last chapter how recessions and inflation can arise because aggregate demand is less or greater than aggregate supply, it is interesting to note than in a barter economy these difficulties would not occur. If every act of supplying is simultaneously an act of demanding an equivalent value, then when we add up the value of all the goods and services supplied and demanded in a barter economy they will always be exactly the same. No depressions or recessions. No demand pull inflation. It's enough to make one wonder who was the idiot who dreamed up the idea of money!

Sometimes ideas that seem good at the time turn out to cause more trouble than they're worth. Maybe finding some object that everyone agrees to accept in exchange for goods or services was just one of those lousy ideas that looked good until it was too late to do anything about it. But let's think more before jumping to conclusions. Barter exchange seemed to do the job well enough in the above example. But what if I want potatoes and carrots in my stew, as before, but my carrot growing neighbor wants carrots and onions in her stew, and my onion growing neighbor wants onions and potatoes in her stew? We would have to arrange some kind of three cornered trade. I could not trade potatoes for carrots because my carrot growing neighbor doesn't want potatoes. My carrot growing neighbor could not trade carrots for onions because the onion grower doesn't want carrots. And the onion growing neighbor could not trade her onions for my potatoes because I don't want onions. I could trade potatoes for onions -- which I don't really want -- except to trade the onions for carrots. Or, my carrot growing neighbor could trade carrots for potatoes she doesn't want, except to trade the potatoes for onions. Or, my onion growing neighbor could trade onions for carrots she doesn't want, except to trade for potatoes. But arranging mutually beneficial deals obviously becomes more problematic when there are even three goods, much less thousands.

There are two problems with barter exchange when there are more than two goods: (1) Not all the mutually beneficial, multiparty deals might be discovered -- which would be a shame since it means people wouldn't always get to eat their stew the way they want it. And, (2) even if a mutually beneficial multiparty deal is discovered and struck, what economists call the *transaction costs* in time, guarantees, and assurances might be considerable. Money eliminates both these problems. As long as all three of us agree to exchange our vegetables for money there is no need to work out complicated three-cornered trades. Each of us simply sells our vegetable for money to whomever wants to buy it, and then uses the money we got to buy whatever vegetable we want.

Simple. No complicated contracts. No lawyers needed. But notice that now it *is* possible to supply without simultaneously demanding an equivalent value. When I sell my potatoes for money I have contributed to supply without contributing to demand. Of course, if I turn around and use all the money I got from selling my potatoes to buy carrots for my stew I will have contributed as much to demand as I did to supply when you consider the two transactions together. But money separates the acts of supplying and demanding, making it *possible* to do one without doing the other. Suppose I come and sell my potatoes for money and then my six year old breaks his arm running around underneath the vegetable stands, I take him to the emergency room, and by the time we get back to the vegetable market it's closed. In this case I will have added to the supply in the Saturday vegetable market without adding to the demand.

Nobody is seriously concerned about this problem in simple vegetable markets, but in large capitalist economies the fact that monetized exchange makes possible discrepancies between supply and demand in the aggregate can be problematic. Once a business has paid for inputs and hired labor they have every incentive to sell their product. But if the price they must settle for leaves a profit that is negative, unacceptable, or just disappointing, the business may well wait for better market conditions before using the proceeds from the sale to purchase more inputs and labor to produce again. The specter of workers anxious to work going without jobs because employers don't believe they will be able to sell what those workers would produce is a self-fulfilling prophesy that tens of millions of victims of the Great Depression of the 1930s, and more recently the Great Recession of 2008, can attest is no mere theoretical concern!

Bigamy - Not a Proper Marriage between Lenders and Borrowers

What if there were no banks? How would people who want to spend more than their income, i.e. borrow, meet people who wish to spend less than their income, i.e. lend? How would businesses with profitable investment opportunities in excess of their retained earnings meet households willing to loan them their savings? If banks did not exist there would be sections in the classified advertisements in newspapers, or listings on ebay, titled "loan wanted" and "willing to loan." But matching would-be borrowers with would-be lenders is not a simple process. These ads might not be as titillating as personals, but they would have to go into details such as: "Want to lend $4,500 for three years with quarterly payments at 9.5% annual rate of interest to credit worthy customer -- references required." And, "Want to borrow 2 million dollars to finance construction of eight, half million dollar homes on prime suburban land already purchased. Willing to pay 7.5% over thirty years. Well known developer with over fifty years of successful business activity in the area." But matching lenders and borrowers in this way entails two kinds of transaction costs. First, the credit worthiness of borrowers is not easy to determine. Particularly small lenders don't want to spend time checking on references of loan applicants. Second, not all mutually beneficial deals are between a single lender and borrower. Many mutually beneficial deals are multiparty swaps. Searching through ads to find all mutually beneficial, multiparty deals takes time -- more than most people have -- and guaranteeing the commitments and terms of multiparty deals takes time and legal expertise. One way to understand what banks do is to see them as "match makers" for borrowers and lenders. But it turns out they are more than efficient match makers who reduce transaction costs by informational economies of scale.

Perhaps banks could perform their service like the match maker in *Fiddler on the Roof* -- collecting fees from the lender and borrower when they marry -- but they don't. Banks don't introduce borrowers and lenders who then contract a "proper" marriage between themselves. Instead, banks engage in legalized bigamy! A bank "marries" its depositors -- paying interest on deposits which depositors can redeem on demand. Then the bank "marries" its loan customers -- who pay interest on loans which the bank can only redeem on specified future dates. But notice that if both the bank's "spouses" insist on exercising their full legal rights, no bank would be able to fulfill its legal obligations. If depositors exercise their legal right to withdraw all their deposits, and if loan customers refuse to pay back their loans any faster than their loan contracts require, every bank would immediately be insolvent. It is only because not all spouses with whom banks engage in bigamy choose to simultaneously exercise their full legal rights that banks can get away with bigamy -- and make a handsome profit for themselves in the process.

Many depositors assume when they deposit money in their checking account the bank simply puts their money into a safe, along with all the other deposits, where it sits until they choose to withdraw it. After all, unless it is all kept available there is no way the bank could give all depositors all their money back if they asked for it. But if that is what banks did they could never make any loans, and therefore they could never make any profits! To assume banks hold all the deposits they accept is to think banks offer a kind of collective safety deposit box service for cash. But that is not at all what banks offer when they accept deposits. Banks use those deposits to make loans to customers who pay the bank interest. As long as the bank collects interest on loans that is higher on average than the interest the bank pays depositors, banks can make a profit. But to realize the potential profit from the difference between the loan and deposit rates of interest, banks have to loan the deposits. And if they loan even a small part of the deposits, obviously not all the deposits can be there in the eventuality that depositors ask to withdraw all their money.

Which leads to a frightening realization: *Banks inherently entail the possibility of bankruptcy.* There is no way to guarantee that banks will always be able to honor their legal commitments to depositors without making it impossible for banks to make profits. That is, no matter how safe and conservative bank management, no matter how faithfully borrowers repay bank loans, depositors are inherently at risk. But the logic of banking is even worse, which is why every government on the planet regulates the banking industry in ways no other industry is subjected to.

How can a bank increase its profits? Profits will be higher if the differential between the rates of interest paid on loans and on deposits is larger. Every bank would like to expand this differential, but how can they? If a bank starts charging higher interest on loans it will risk losing its loan customers to other banks. If it offers to pay less on deposits it risks losing depositors to other banks. In other words, individual banks are limited by competition with other banks from expanding the differential beyond a certain point. Another way of saying the same thing is that the size of the differential is determined by the amount of competition in the banking industry. If there is lots of competition the differential will be small, if there is less competition the differential will be larger. But for a given level of competition, individual banks are restricted in their ability to increase profits by expanding their own differential. The other determinant of bank profits is how many loans they make taking advantage of the differential. If a bank loans out 40% of its deposits and earns $X in profits, it could earn $2X profits by lending out 80% of its deposits. Since there is little an individual bank can do to expand its interest differential, banks concentrate on loaning out as much of their deposits as possible.

Which leads to a second frightening realization: *When stockholders press bank officers to increase profits, bank CEOs are driven to loan out more and more of bank deposits and keep less as reserves.* Since insolvency results when depositors ask to withdraw more than the bank has kept as reserves, the drive for more profits necessarily increases the likelihood of bankruptcy by lowering bank reserves. It is true that stockholders should seek a tradeoff between higher profits and greater risk of insolvency since shareholders lose the value of their investment if the bank they own goes bankrupt. But stockholders are not the only ones who lose when a bank goes bankrupt. While stockholders lose the value of their investment, depositors lose their deposits. So when stockholders weigh the benefit of higher profits against the expected cost of bankruptcy they do not weigh the benefits against the entire cost, but only the fraction of the cost that falls on them. And even with regulations requiring minimum capitalization, it is always the case that the cost of bankruptcy to depositors is much greater than the cost to shareholders. This means that the interests of bank shareholders do not coincide with the public interest in finding the efficient tradeoff between higher profitability and lower likelihood of insolvency. *Hence the need for government regulation.*

This was a lesson that history taught over and over again during the eighteenth and nineteenth centuries as periodic waves of bankruptcy rocked the growing American Republic. Early in the twentieth century Congress charged the Federal Reserve Bank with the task of setting and enforcing a *minimum legal reserve requirement* that prevents banks from lending out more than a certain fraction of their deposits. In 1933 Congress also created a federal agency to insure depositors in the eventuality of bankruptcy in its efforts to reassure the public that it was safe to deposit their savings in banks during the Great Depression. Today the Federal Deposit Insurance Corporation (FDIC) will fully redeem individual deposits up to $200,000 in value if a bank goes bankrupt.

But federal insurance has created two new problems. First of all, as we discovered in the Savings and Loan Crisis of the 1980's, any substantial string of bankruptcies will also bankrupt the insuring agency. When the Savings and Loan Crisis was finally recognized there were roughly 500 insolvent thrift institutions with deposits of over $200 billion. The Federal Savings and Loan Insurance Corporation, FSLIC, had less than $2 billion in assets at the time. Federal insurance also aggravates what economists call *moral hazard* in the banking sector. Bank owners and large depositors can essentially collude in placing and accepting deposits in financial institutions that pay high interest on deposits which are used to make risky loans that pay high returns -- as long as the borrowers don't default. But when there are defaults on risky loans neither depositors nor shareholders are the major victims of insolvency and bankruptcy. Lightly capitalized shareholders lose little in case of bankruptcy, while fully insured depositors lose nothing. Meanwhile both have been enjoying high returns while running little or no risk in the process. So government insurance compounds the problem that bank officers cannot be counted on to pursue the public interest in an efficient tradeoff between profitability and risk by no longer making it necessary for depositors to monitor the lending activities of the financial institutions where they place their deposits.

The much discussed problem known as *too big to fail* is an extension of this problem. When the US Congress balked at Treasury Secretary Hank Paulson Sr.'s request in the fall of 2008 to appropriate $700 billion for his Troubled Assets Relief Program, TARP -- pointing out that asking the US taxpayer to bail out the banks whose reckless behavior had caused the financial crisis hardly seemed fair – Paulson famously explained to them in congressional testimony that they were "already on the hook," since failure to do so would cause US citizens far greater damage. What Paulson pointed out was that as long as any bank was so large that permitting it to fail would rock the financial sector, that bank could engage in reckless behavior knowing full well that the government would have to bail it out at taxpayers' expense.

Finally, notice that the existence of banks means the functioning money supply is considerably larger than the amount of currency circulating in the economy. If we ask how much someone could buy, immediately, in a world without banks the answer would be the amount of currency that person has. But in a world with banks, where sellers not only accept currency in exchange for goods and services, but accept checks drawn on banks as well, someone can buy an amount equal to the currency they have *plus* the balance they have in their checking account. This means the "functioning" money supply is equal to the amount of currency circulating in the economy *plus* the sum total balances in household and business bank accounts of various kinds – which are many times larger than the amount of currency in circulation.

Which leads to our last frightening realization. *Most of the functioning money supply is literally created by private commercial banks when they accept deposits and make loans.* But as we have seen, when banks engage in these activities, and thereby "create most of the functioning money supply, they think only of their own profits and give nary a thought to the sacred public trust of preserving the integrity of "money" in our economy.

Monetary Policy

In chapter 4 we learned how fiscal policy -- changes in government spending or taxes -- can be used to increase aggregate demand to reduce unemployment gaps, or decrease aggregate demand to reduce inflation gaps. Monetary policy provides an alternative way to increase or decrease aggregate demand.

The Federal Reserve Bank -- called the Central Bank in other countries -- can change the supply of money in the economy in several ways we needn't go into. An increase in the money supply will reduce interest rates, while a decrease in the money supply will raise interest rates. Higher interest rates increase the cost of borrowing for businesses considering how much to invest in new projects. While lower interest rates decrease the cost of borrowing, and predictably increases investment spending by the business sector, leading to even larger increases in overall aggregate demand and therefore equilibrium GDP. Just like fiscal policy, monetary policy can be either expansionary – raising aggregate demand and equilibrium GDP to combat unemployment -- or deflationary – reducing aggregate demand and equilibrium GDP to combat demand pull inflation.

The Relationship between the Real and Financial Economies

All too often the economic "news" reported in the media is about what is happening in the financial sector. During the stock market boom in the late 1990s the media often acted like cheer leaders for the Dow Jones Average and NASDAQ index -- reporting with glee that stock prices rose dramatically after a Labor Department briefing announced an increase in the number of jobless -- even though the rise in unemployment clearly meant that the economy was becoming *less* efficient! What should we care about, and what is the relationship between the financial sector and the "real" economy?

The three chapters that follow address the question: What should we demand from our economy? The answer is that we want scarce productive resources, including our own labor, to be used efficiently. We want the natural environment to be used sustainably. And we want the burdens and benefits of economic activity to be distributed equitably. Nowhere on this "wish list" do rising stock prices, bond yields, or currency values appear. This does not mean the financial sector has nothing to do with the production and distribution of goods and services. But it does mean the only reason to care about the financial sector is because of its effects on the real economy. If the financial sector improves economic efficiency and thereby allows us to produce more goods and services, so much the better. But if dynamics in the financial sector cause unemployment and lost production, or increase economic injustice, or hasten environmental deterioration, *that* is what matters, not the fact that a stock index or currency rose or fell in value. In an era when the hegemony of global finance is unprecedented, it is important not to invert what matters and what is only of derivative interest.

How can money, lending, banks, hedge funds, options, buying on margin, derivatives, or credit default swaps increase economic efficiency? Simple: By providing funding for some productive activity in the real economy that otherwise would not have taken place. If monetized exchange allows people to discover a mutually beneficial deal they would have been unlikely to find through barter, money increases the efficiency of the real economy. If I can borrow from you to buy a tool that allows me to work more productively right away, whereas otherwise I would have had to save for a year to buy the tool, a credit market increases my efficiency this year -- and the interest rate you and I agree on will distribute the increase in *my* productivity during the year between you, the lender, and me, the borrower. If banks permit more borrowers and lenders to find one another, thereby allowing more people to work more productively sooner than they otherwise would have, the banking system increases efficiency in the real economy. If options, buying on margin, credit default swaps, and derivatives mobilize savings that otherwise would have been idle, and extend credit to borrowers who become more productive sooner than had they been forced to wait longer for loans from more traditional sources in the credit system, these financial innovations increase efficiency in the real economy.

However, while those who profit from the financial system are quick to point out these *positive* potentials, they seldom point out ways the financial sector can *negatively* impact the real economy. Nor do they dwell on the fact that what the credit system allows creditors to do is profit from increases in the productivity of their debtors.

At its best what the credit systems does, in all its different guises, is allow lenders to appropriate increases in the productivity of others. Why do those whose productivity rises agree to pay creditors part of their productivity increase? Because the creditors have the wealth needed to purchase whatever is necessary to increase their productivity while they do not. Moreover, if they wait until they can save sufficient wealth to do without creditors, borrowers lose whatever efficiency gain they could have produced in the meantime.

Banks, futures, options, margins, derivatives, credit default swaps and other "financial innovations" all either expand the list of ways that creditors can lend to debtors, or permit creditors to increase their *leverage* -- use less of their own wealth and more of someone else's when they lend or invest. In other words these, and whatever new financial instruments speculators dream up in the future, simply extend the credit system. If the extension provides funding for some productive activity that would otherwise not have been funded, it can be useful.

But what is too often ignored is that all extensions increase dangers in the credit system by:

- Increasing the number of places something might go wrong.

- Increasing the probability that if something does go wrong, investors will panic and the credit system will crash.

- Compounding the damage when the credit system does crash.

New financial products add new markets where bubbles can form and burst.

Increased leverage makes financial structures more fragile and compounds the damage from any bubble that does burst. There are two rules of behavior in any credit system, and both rules become more critical to follow the more leveraged the system.

*Rule #1 is the rule all participants want all **other** participants to follow:* DON'T PANIC!

If everyone follows rule #1 the likelihood of the credit system crashing is lessened.

*Rule #2 is the rule each participant must be careful to follow **herself**:* PANIC FIRST!

If something goes wrong, the first to collect her loan from a debtor in trouble, the first to withdraw her deposits from a troubled bank, the first to sell her option or derivative in a market when a bubble bursts, the first to dump a foreign currency when it is "under pressure," will lose the least. While those who are slow to panic will suffer the largest losses.

Once stated, the contradictory nature of the two logical rules for behavior in credit systems make clear the inherent danger in this powerful economic institution, and the risk we take when we tie the real economy ever more tightly to a credit system which the financial industry and politicians have conspired to make more unstable and fragile over the past four decades.

PART TWO: NORMATIVE ECONOMICS

While positive economics concentrates on understanding how the economy works and predicting what *will* happen, *normative economics* focuses on *evaluating* how well the economy is performing. The three chapters to follow explain how to answer the following questions:

6. Is our labor being used efficiently?

7. Are we adequately protecting the natural environment?

8. Are the burdens and benefits of economic activity being distributed fairly?

6 GETTING THE MOST FROM OUR WORK

So far we have simply explored what will happen in a capitalist economy with particular technologies. What will prices, wage, profit, and rental rates be? How large will overall production or actual GDP be? All this is called *positive economics*. What economists call *normative economics* goes on to evaluate outcomes, i.e. tries to distinguish between outcomes which are more desirable from others which are less so. In what ways might some outcomes be better or worse than others?

We have already tiptoed into normative economics by assuming that it is better if the economy is producing up to its potential, and that government fiscal and monetary policies which bring actual GDP closer to potential GDP improve economic performance. But what else should we demand from the economy?

- As long as labor is more burdensome or less pleasurable than leisure, working more hours to produce the same amount of any good is undesirable.

- Once nature is no longer "abundant," reducing stocks of natural resources, or using up scarce storage capacity in environmental sinks is undesirable.

- And finally, it is undesirable if the burdens and benefits of economic activity are distributed unfairly among participants.

In other words, outcomes which use our labor more *efficiently*, are more *environmentally sustainable*, and are more *equitable* are better than outcomes which are less so.

Our simple two good model permits us to determine when we will economize on use of our labor, when we will economize on our use of the natural environment, and when we will not. We address how to measure when we are using our labor efficiently, when we are likely to do so, and when we are not, in this chapter, and address environmental sustainability in chapter 7. In chapter 8 we introduce a new model to facilitate discussion of what is fair, and explore when fair outcomes are likely to be achieved.

Labor Time "Values"

How many hours does it take to produce a unit of good 1? At first it seems like we already have the answer, L(1), which in the example we have been using is 1 hour. But it also takes a(11) = .3 units of good 1 and a(21) = .2 units of good 2 to produce one unit of good 1, and it takes some labor to produce those inputs. So while it only takes 1 hour of labor *directly* to produce a unit of good 1, it must take more than one hour *directly* **and** *indirectly* to produce a unit of good 1 when we account for the labor it takes to produce the other inputs needed. Similarly, the total hours of labor it takes to make a unit of good 2 is not only the direct labor, L(2) = .5 hours, but also the number of hours it takes to make a(12) = .2 units of good 1 and a(22) = .4 units of good 2, which are also needed to produce one unit of good 2.

Define V(j) as the number of hours of labor needed **both directly and indirectly** *to make a unit of good j.* In other words, define V(1) and V(2) as the answers we are seeking. Now ask: How many hours both directly and indirectly did it take to make a(ij) units of good i ? By definition it takes V(i) hours in grand sum total to make 1 unit of good i. So it must take V(i)a(ij) hours in total to make a(ij) units of good i. We can now write the *labor time equations* for the economy:

(6) V(1) = L(1) + V(1)a(11) + V(2)a(21)
(7) V(2) = L(2) + V(1)a(12) + V(2)a(22)

The first equation says: The number of hours it takes in grand sum total to make 1 unit of good 1, V(1), equals the hours of direct labor, L(1) -- stirring time, if you will -- plus the number of hours it took to make a(11) units of good 1, plus the number of hours it took to make a(21) units of good 2 – i.e. the time it took to make the ingredients. The second equation says the same for good 2. Since all of the a(ij)s and L(j)s are "givens," i.e. they are simply the description of the technologies being used, there are only two unknowns, V(1) and V(2). While we cannot solve equation 1 without knowing the value for V(2), and we cannot solve equation 2 without knowing the value of V(1), we can solve the two equations simultaneously to obtain mutually consistent values for V(1) and V(2). The important points are:

- The technological data -- the a(ij)s and L(j)s -- are sufficient to calculate the labor time values in our economy.

- We would like these labor time values to be as *small* as possible, i.e. we would like to work as few hours as possible to produce a unit of each good.

Substituting the numerical values we have been using in our example into our labor time equations gives:

$V(1) = 1 + .3V(1) + .2V(2)$
$V(2) = .5 + .2V(1) + .4V(2)$

Which can be solved to give: $V(1) = 1.84211$, the number of hours of labor it takes both directly and indirectly to produce a unit of good 1, and $V(2) = 1.44737$, the number of hours of labor it takes both directly and indirectly to produce a unit of good 2.[8]

So far we have been assuming there is only one way to make each good. But there is often more than one *technique*, or recipe, available. R&D departments are constantly searching for new techniques, or recipes. We would like our economy to economize on use of our labor, i.e. we want the economy to use the technique with the lowest labor time value. Capitalists presumably will use whatever technique has the lowest unit production cost.

Adam Smith's Invisible Hand

Long ago in his famous treatise *The Wealth of Nations*, Adam Smith hypothesized that there is a *one-to-one correspondence* between techniques which reduce capitalist production costs and techniques which reduce labor time values. Smith explained that it was as if capitalists were "guided by an invisible hand" to adopt all techniques which reduce labor time values, not because they wished to serve the social interest by doing so, but because they would reduce the capitalist's own production costs. And similarly, capitalists would be "guided by an invisible hand" to reject any techniques which increase labor time values, not because they wished to serve the

---

[8] As before, you can use https://www.wolframalpha.com to solve these two equations.

social interest, but because they would raise the capitalist's own production costs. It turns out that the situation is somewhat more complicated. Over two hundred years after the publication of *The Wealth of Nations,* John Roemer demonstrated that Adam Smith's hypothesis was only partially correct. Roemer proved that only in the special case where the rate of profit is zero does Smith's fortuitous, one-to-one correspondence hold. Moreover, Roemer proved that the higher the rate of profit, the greater the discrepancy between cost reducing and labor time reducing technologies becomes.[9]

We can illustrate the problem Roemer discovered as follows: Back in chapter 3 we calculated that for the initial technologies, setting $p(2) = 1$:

$a(11) = 0.3 \quad a(12) = 0.2$
$a(21) = 0.2 \quad a(22) = 0.4$
$L(1) = 1.0 \quad L(2) = 0.5$

(A) When $r = 0$, $w = .690909$ and $p(1) = 1.27273$. (B) When $r = .12604$, $w = .500$ and $p(1) = 1.19034$. And (C) when $r = .20847$, $w = .400$ and $p(1) = 1.13746$. What would a capitalist in industry 1 do if his R&D department came up with the following new technique for making good 1 which used more of good 2 as an input but fewer hours of labor:[10]

$a(11)' = .3 = .3 = a(11)$
$a(21)' = .3 > .2 = a(21)$
$L(1)' = .8 < 1.0 = L(1)$

In situation A the capitalist in industry 1 would compare the cost of producing a unit of good 1 using the old and new technologies as follows:

---

[9] See theorems 4.9 and 4.10 in John Roemer, *Analytical Foundations of Marxian Economic Theory* (Cambridge UK: Cambridge University Press, 1979).

[10] Because $a(21)' > a(21)$, this new technique is often referred to as "capital using" or CU. And because $L(1)' < L(1)$ it is also referred to as "labor saving," or LS. However, whether this, or any CU-LS new technique reduces the amount of labor needed directly *and* indirectly to produce a unit of good 1 is not a foregone conclusion. Remember that $L(1)$ is not the same as $V(1)$. So whether $V(1)'$ is larger or smaller than $V(1)$ remains to be seen.

Old cost:
p(1)a(11)+p(2)a(21)+wL(1) = 1.27273(.3)+1(.2) +.690909(1)=1.27278

New cost:
p(1)a(11)'+p(2)a(21)'+wL(1)'=1.27273(.3)+1(.3)+.690909(.8)=1.23455

And since the cost per unit of output is *lower* using the new technology, a profit maximizing capitalist would *adopt* it in an economy where the rate of profit is zero. Moreover, unless the capitalist could patent the new technique and thereby prevent other capitalists producing good 1 from using it, they would all quickly adopt the new technique to avoid being competed out of business by the capitalist whose R&D department first discovered it, and who now has the advantage of lower production costs. Consequently, the new technique would become the one used by all capitalists in industry 1.

In situation C the capitalist in industry 1 whose R&D department came up with the new technique would compare the cost of producing a unit of good 1 using the old and new technologies as follows:

Old cost:
p(1)a(11)+p(2)a(21)+wL(1) = 1.13746(.3)+1(.2)+.400(1) = .941238

New cost:
p(1)a(11)'+p(2)a(21)'+wL(1)' = 1.13746(.3)+1(.3)+.400(.8) = .961238

And since the cost per unit of output is *higher* using the new technology, a profit maximizing capitalist would *reject* it in an economy where the profit rate is 20.847%, and all capitalists in industry 1 would continue to produce good 1 using the old technology.

What remains to be determined is if adopting the new CU-LS technique reduces or increases labor time values. In the old economy we calculated that the labor time values were V(1) = 1.84211 hours of labor needed both directly and indirectly to produce a unit of good 1, and V(2) = 1.44737 hours of labor needed both directly and indirectly to produce a unit of good 2. If all capitalists in the first industry adopted the new technique the labor time equations for the economy would become:

$V(1)' = .8 + .3V(1)' + .3V(2)'$
$V(2)' = .5 + .2V(1)' + .4V(2)'$

Which gives $V(1)' = 1.75000$ and $V(2)' = 1.41667$ – both of which are *lower* than the corresponding labor time values for the old economy.[11] This means that it is efficient and socially beneficial to adopt the new technique for producing good 1, and abandon the old, less efficient technique, because we will have to work fewer hours to get a unit of *both* goods if it is adopted. In which case, it appears that capitalists can be relied on to serve the social interest in situation A – where the rate of profit in the economy is zero. However, in situation C, when the rate of profit is 20.847%, profit maximizing capitalists in industry 1 apparently will subvert the social interest by rejecting the new technique *even though it reduces the amount of labor time it takes to produce both goods*. How can we explain this conundrum?

To solve the puzzle we start with what we know: We now know the new technology in our example made the economy more efficient. We know the new technology was capital-using and labor-saving, CU-LS. And we know capitalists in industry 1 embraced it when the wage rate was .690909 (and the rate of profit was zero), but rejected it when the wage rate was .400000 (and the rate of profit was 20.847%.) The reason for capitalists' seemingly contradictory behavior is now clear: In situation A when the wage rate is higher, the savings in labor cost because the new technology is labor-saving was greater -- and great enough to outweigh the increase in non-labor cost because the new technology is capital-using. But in situation C when the wage rate is lower, the savings in labor cost is less, and no longer out weights the increase in non-labor cost. Apparently the price signals {p(1), p(2), and w} in the economy in case A lead capitalists to make the socially useful choice to adopt the new, more productive technology, whereas different price signals in case C lead capitalists to make the socially counterproductive choice to reject the new, more productive technology.

No matter how efficient, or socially productive a new CU-LS technology

---

[11] Since the technique used to produce good 2 has not changed, it might seem odd that the labor time value for good 2 has changed. But notice that .2 units of good 1 are used to produce a unit of good 2, and since it now takes fewer hours to produce a unit of good 1 because $V(1)' < V(1)$, it will take fewer hours indirectly to produce good 2 as well.

may be, it is clear that if the wage rate is low enough (because the rate of profit is high enough) such an efficient technology will become cost-increasing, rather than cost-reducing, and capitalists will reject it. Similarly, no matter how inefficient, or socially counterproductive a new CS-LU technology may be, if the wage rate is low enough (because the rate of profit is high enough) the inefficient technology will become cost-reducing, rather than cost-increasing, and capitalists will embrace it.

In other words, while Adam Smith's invisible hand works perfectly when the rate of profit is zero, it cannot be relied on when the rate of profit is greater than zero. Moreover, as the rate of profit rises (and consequently the wage rate falls), the likelihood that socially efficient CU-LS technologies will be rejected, and the likelihood that socially counterproductive CS-LU technologies will be adopted by profit maximizing capitalists increases.

7 PRESERVING THE NATURAL ENVIRONMENT

The appropriate coefficients for inputs from the natural environment when deriving prices, wages, and rents are not always the appropriate coefficients when measuring *environmental throughput*, the amount of some scarce natural resource or some scarce environmental sink capacity that is used up in production.

Calculating Environmental Throughput

For example, suppose the input from the natural environment is land, measured in acres, and suppose that after a farmer uses the land it remains in exactly the same condition as it was initially. The farmer may well pay rent to a landowner to use the land even though it does not diminish in size, or by hypothesis deteriorate in any way. In which case, in the example from chapter 3, if the farmer produces one unit of good 1 on this land she will need to have .3 acres available and will have to pay .3u in rent. But notice that in this case environmental throughput is zero by hypothesis. On the other hand suppose the input from the natural environment is fresh water drawn from an aquifer. In this case the farmer will diminish the aquifer by .3 gallons when she produces a unit of good 1. So in this case water throughput is .3 gallons.

When calculating environmental throughput we need the coefficients in our production technologies to represent the amount that the stock of a natural resource, or the storage capacity of a natural sink, is diminished -- which may sometimes correspond with the amount which must be on hand and available for use, but in some cases, as just explained, may not. In truth what we care about is how much any "environmental service" deteriorates when goods are produced, but it is common to think of this in terms of reducing scarce stocks of natural resources or depleting the storage capacity of environmental sinks.

To make this distinction we will use the letter T to represent input coefficients for **t**hroughput from the natural environment, whereas we used the letter N to represent the quantity of a primary resource from **n**ature that must be on hand for production. For simplicity we begin by assuming that nature is homogeneous, i.e. there is only one input from nature, just as we began by abstracting from differences between carpentry, welding, and computer programming labor and assumed labor is homogeneous. Suppose our production technologies, which now have throughput consequences, are those below:

$a(11) = 0.3 \quad a(12) = 0.2$
$a(21) = 0.2 \quad a(22) = 0.4$
$L(1) = 1.0 \quad L(2) = 0.5$
$T(1) = 0.2 \quad T(2) = 0.1$

We can calculate the amount of environmental throughput used up, both directly and indirectly, when we produce a unit of each good in exactly the same way we calculated how many hours of labor it takes, both directly and indirectly, to produce a unit of each good. In short, we must account for the fact that to produce a unit of good 1, for example, it also requires some throughput to produce the a(11) and a(21) we need, just as we took into account that it requires some labor to produce a(11) and a(21) when we calculated the labor time value, V(1). Define H(1) *as the amount of throughput used, both directly and indirectly, when we produce a unit of good 1, and H(2) similarly.* Our "throughput equations" are:

(8) H(1) = T(1) + H(1)a(11) + H(2)a(21)
(9) H(2) = T(2) + H(1)a(12) + H(2)a(22)

Substituting in the coefficients in our example:

$H(1) = .2 + .3H(1) + .2H(2)$
$H(2) = .1 + .2H(1) + .4H(2)$

Which can be solved to give H(1) = .368421 and H(2) = .289474, the amounts of throughput from the environment "used up" both directly and indirectly when we produce one unit of good 1 and good 2 respectively.[12] And if during a year we produce X(1) units of good 1 and X(2) units of good 2, *environmental throughput, ET,* will be: ET = H(1)X(1)+H(2)X(2) = .368421X(1)+.289474X(2).

---

[12] As always, you can use https://www.wolframalpha.com to solve these equations.

Environmental Sustainability

For simplicity assume the economy is initially environmentally sustainable, i.e. the number of units of nature used up by production each year is exactly equal to the number of units which regenerate naturally each year. In which case, if technologies do not change, if the labor force does not grow, and if the number of hours worked in each industry does not change, output and throughput will remain constant, throughput will continue to equal regeneration year after year, and the economy will remain *environmentally sustainable*.

But what if we discover and adopt new technologies which increase labor productivity and continue to work the same number of hours in each industry? This will increase economic wellbeing because we will get more goods for the same amount of work, but it will also increase output and therefore environmental throughput. In this scenario the only way the economy can remain environmentally sustainable is if technological change also increases throughput efficiency. In other words, loosely speaking, if the X's in our above expression for annual environmental throughput, ET, increase because of increases in labor productivity, the H's in the expression must decrease to the same extent to preserve environmental sustainability. Or, if we think about increases in labor productivity as decreases in labor time values, V's, and we think about increases in throughput efficiency as decreases in environmental throughput "values," H's, then if hours worked in each industry remain constant, as long as the H's are shrinking as fast as the V's, throughput will remain unchanged.[13]

So, contrary to what many in the steady-state economy and de-growth

---

[13] We can be even more precise: Theorem 18 in *Income Distribution and Environmental Sustainability* provides a precise way to measure quantitatively how much any technological change introduced in a multi-good economy increases labor productivity, $\varrho(l)$. And theorem 20 provides a precise way to measure quantitatively how much any technological change introduced in the economy increases environmental throughput efficiency, $\varrho(n)$. If hours worked in all industries remains the same, as long as all technical changes introduced in the economy during a year *collectively* increase throughput efficiency by as much as they increase labor productivity, environmental throughput will remain constant.

movements seem to believe: *Even if we continue to work the same number of hours in every industry – that is even if we take none of any increase in labor productivity in the form of leisure, and even if we do not substitute less throughput intensive goods for more throughput intensive goods in consumption -- it is possible to increase labor productivity, and therefore output per capita and economic wellbeing, without putting greater strain on the environment* **as long as throughput efficiency grows as fast as labor productivity.**

In short, environmental sustainability reduces to whether or not increases in throughput efficiency keep pace with increases in labor productivity, or, as environmental economists put it, on whether or not we can sufficiently *decouple* growth of output from growth of throughput.

It is easy to motivate the impression that this is impossible – that when output of goods increases environmentally damaging throughput must increase as well -- by pointing out that this has, in fact, historically been the case under capitalism to date. But that is (a) obvious to anyone who recognizes that we have been exhausting the environment and need to stop before it is too late, and (b) completely irrelevant to whether or not this must necessarily continue to be the case.

Take greenhouse gas emissions for example: For the period from 1960 to 2000 real global gross domestic product grew at 2.7% per year, but global greenhouse gas emissions grew only at 1.3% per year *because greenhouse gas throughput efficiency increased by 1.4% per year.* However, what scientists are telling us is that unless greenhouse gas throughput falls dramatically, i.e. unless increases in greenhouse gas throughput efficiency outstrip increases in real gross domestic product considerably, we are headed for climate disaster by mid-century. Which is why the fact that global greenhouse gas throughput efficiency only increased by 0.7% from 2000 to 2014 is worrisome, but the fact that it has started to rise again in the past few years is somewhat encouraging. Nonetheless, increasing greenhouse gas throughput efficiency is clearly possible. And if we can increase it enough it is perfectly consistent with continued increases in global gross domestic product. We just need much, much greater increases in greenhouse gas throughput efficiency. As a matter of fact, we need a crash program, or as some now call it, a *Green New Deal*, to reduce fossil fuels in the energy mix and increase energy efficiency in industry, agriculture, transportation, and housing.

In any case, the good news is that if we increase environmental throughput efficiency we can also increase labor productivity, and the economic wellbeing this brings, at that same rate, without any increase in environmental throughput. However, this should not be misinterpreted as denying the importance of substituting more leisure for less consumption and shifting consumption toward less throughput intensive goods and services. Nor does it mean there is not an unhealthy and environmentally destructive growth imperative in today's economies. It just means we must go beyond facile arguments which, upon inspection, prove not to be compelling, to explain why this is the case.[14][15]

---

[14] See Part II, "Why the Environment is at Risk," in Robin Hahnel, *Green Economics: Confronting the Ecological Crisis*. (White Plains, NY: M.E. Sharpe, 2012) for discussion of specific ways in which today's economies tend to generate an unhealthy and environmentally unsustainable "growth imperative."

[15] It is obvious that the environment differs in at least two important ways from our simplifying assumptions in this chapter: (1)There are many *different* natural resources and sinks which we must be concerned with. And (2) some of them do not regenerate, i.e. they are *not* reproducible. For a discussion of how this complicates matters see section 2.6 in *Income Distribution and Environmental Sustainability*. Nonetheless, even in a context where there are many different inputs from the natural environment and some are not reproducible, the conclusion that infinite growth in labor productivity, output per capita, and therefore economic wellbeing is theoretically impossible "on a finite planet" proves to be *un*warranted.

8 DISTRIBUTIVE JUSTICE

What is a fair distribution of the burdens and benefits of economic activity? Is a private enterprise, market economy likely to achieve a fair distribution, or deviate from fair outcomes in some predictable way? Ultimately *distributive justice* is a philosophical matter, but before delving into philosophical issues we use our simple model to flag a nagging concern, and elaborate a new model to help explore important dilemmas that arise in debates over distributive justice.

In the model in chapter 3 we found that if the hourly wage rate is .690909 units of good 2 per hour, the price of good 1 will be 1.27273 units of good 2 and the rate of profit will be zero. In which case those who work to produce goods will get *all* the surplus good 1 -- .5 units -- and *all* the surplus good 2 -- .4 units – they produce. And their employers, who do no work, will receive nothing. On the other hand, if the hourly wage rate is .5 units of good 2 per hour the rate of profit will be 12.6%, and if the wage rate is .4 units of good 2 per hour, the rate of profit will be 20.8%. In either of these latter cases those who do all the work to produce everything do *not* get all the surplus goods they produce, *because* their employers who do no work get some of the surplus of good 1 and good 2 produced by their employees. It appears that whenever the rate of profit in the economy is positive, those who show up and work instead of enjoying leisure do not receive all the benefits from the sacrifices they make; while capitalists, who do no work and enjoy 24 hours of leisure every day, receive some of the benefits from sacrifices made by their employees.[16] We might call this the *prima facie* case that positive profits violate distributive justice.

But is it possible that even though capitalists do none of the actual work to produce goods and services, that they do something else for which they deserve compensation? A simple "corn model" can help us understand debates which have long raged over the *morality* of income distribution

---

[16] Note, when a capitalist also shows up to manage the enterprise they own, economists distinguish between a salary for their managerial services and their profits as capitalist. Another way to think of this is that profits are what owners would receive, as capitalists, even if they hired manages and never showed up themselves at the factories they own. In any case, the above result is proved rigorously as theorem 11, which I called the "fundamental Sraffian theorem in *Income Distribution and Environmental Sustainability*.

under capitalism.

A Simple Corn Economy

The economy has 1000 members. There is one produced good, corn. There are two ways to make corn, a *labor intensive technique* (LIT) and a *capital intensive technique* (CIT).

Labor Intensive Technique (LIT):
4 days of labor + 0 units of seed corn "capital" yields 1 bushel of corn
Capital Intensive Technique (CIT):
1 day of labor + 1 unit of seed corn "capital" yields 2 bushels of corn

In either case the corn produced appears at the end of the week, on Sunday. And the bushel of seed corn in the CIT must be available on Monday morning, and is used up by the end of the week. This means that while the *gross output* is 2 bushels of corn per week in the CIT, the *net output* is only 1 bushel.

All members of this society are equally skilled and productive, and all know how to use both the LIT and CIT technologies for producing corn.

It is against the law to work on Saturday and Sunday, so the maximum number of days per week anyone can work is five.

If people use up any seed corn during a week they must replace it.

People must consume 2 bushels of corn every week, and never wish to consume more than 2 bushels in a week. After replacing any seed corn they use up, and after consuming 2 bushels of corn per week, people simply wish to work as few days as possible.

Broadly speaking economic efficiency means maximizing the "gain" we get from the "pain" we endure to get it. In our simple economy "gain" reduces to total net seed corn produced, that is, corn left over after replacing any seed corn used up during production. "Pain" reduces to the total number of days worked to gain net corn. Whenever the ratio of gain to pain increases the economy has become more efficient. So in our simple economy we can calculate how *efficient* the economy is during any week by dividing total net corn produced that week by total days worked that week.

We calculate the degree of *inequality* of any outcome in any week along two dimensions: (1) The most days any individual works minus the least days anyone works that week. (2) The most bushels of seed corn any individual accumulates minus the least bushels anyone accumulates that week. Given our assumption that everyone must consume 2 bushels of corn every week, and does not desire to consume more, there can never be any inequality in consumption.

We calculate *cumulative inequality* along the same two dimensions: (1) the most days any individual has worked in *all* weeks minus the least days any individual has worked in *all* weeks. (2) the most bushels of seed corn any individual has accumulated by the end of any week minus the least bushels of seed corn any individual has accumulated by the end of any week.

Suppose people are not permitted to enter into any economic relationships with one another. What will happen in this economy if, on Monday morning of the first week, everyone starts out with 1 bushel of seed corn?

Week 1: Each person will work all day Monday in the CIT with her bushel of seed corn because she can be much more productive in the CIT than in the LIT. But while this will yield 2 bushels of corn on Sunday, she will have used up her bushel of seed corn, and must use one of the two bushels produced to replace the bushel used up, leaving her with only 1 bushel for consumption. To get the other bushel she needs to consume she will have to work 4 days in the LIT. So each person will work on Monday in the CIT, and on Tuesday through Friday in the LIT, for a grand total of 5 days. Each person will replace her bushel of seed corn, consume 2 bushels of corn, but, given the law against working on Saturday or Sunday, will be unable to accumulate any corn to add to her stock of seed corn for the following week.

Efficiency is: 2000 bushels of net corn produced divided by (5)(1000) = 5000 days worked: 2000/5000 = .40000.
Work inequality is: 5 days − 5 days = 0 days.
Accumulation inequality is: 0 bushels − 0 bushels = 0 bushels.

Week 2: Everyone does the same thing in week 2 she did in week 1. But suppose in week 2, *somehow* 10 extra net bushels are produced, and *somehow* 10 people each end up with 1 extra bushel of corn. Later we will discuss the moral implications of different possible reasons why 10 more bushels are produced, and why 10 people each acquire an extra bushel while the other 990 people do not. But for the time being we remain agnostic about the origin and moral status of the extra bushel which 10 people get in week 2, and confine ourselves to deducing what these 10 people and the other 990 people will do going forward. Meanwhile, in week 2:

Efficiency is: 2010 bushels of net corn produced divided by 5000 days worked: 2010/5000 = .40200.
Work inequality is: 5 days – 5 days = 0 days.
Accumulation inequality is: 1 bushel – 0 bushels = 1 bushel.

Week 3: 990 people have no choice but to continue to do just what they did in weeks 1 and 2. On the other hand, the 10 people who somehow got an extra bushel in week 2 will now have 2 bushels of seed corn at the beginning of week 3,[17] and therefore can work longer in the CIT where their work is more productive than it is in the LIT. The 10 who start week 3 with 2 bushels of seed corn will work Monday and Tuesday in the CIT to produce 4 bushels on Sunday. After replacing the 2 bushels they use up they will have 2 bushels left to consume, and need not work in the LIT at all.

Efficiency is: 2000 bushels of net corn produced divided by (5)(990) + (2)(10) = 4970 days worked: 2000/4970 = .40241.
Work inequality is: 5 days – 2 days = 3 days.
Accumulation inequality is: 0 bushels – 0 bushels = 0 bushels.

At this point it is useful to review where we are. In week 1 outcomes are *equal* for all 1000 people: Everyone works 5 days, replaces any seed corn they use up, consumes 2 bushels of corn, and accumulates no additional seed corn. In

---

[17] Because people do not want to consume more than 2 bushels per week the 10 who got the extra bushel of corn in week 2 will save it and have it available as seed corn to work with in week 3.

week 2 outcomes are *unequal* for some reason yet to be examined. Everyone works 5 days, replaces any seed corn they use up, and consumes 2 bushels of corn. But for some reason 10 people receive an extra bushel of corn in week 2. In week 3 outcomes are also *unequal*, but for a reason we can explain: 10 people work 2 days while 990 people work 5 days *because* 10 people begin week 3 with 2 bushels of seed corn, and therefore can work 2 days in the CIT, while 990 begin week 2 with only 1 bushel, can work only 1 day in the CIT, and must therefore work 4 more days in the LIT.

Efficiency is higher in week 2 than week 1 because 10 more bushels of net corn were produced for some unexplained reason even though everyone worked the same number of days, using the same combination of technologies, as they did in week 1. However, what made the economy more efficient in week 3 than week 1 was not some unexplained event, because in week 3 there was no unexplained event to boost productivity. Instead it was the presence of an extra 10 bushels of seed corn at the beginning of the week which allowed 10 people to each substitute 1 day of work in the CIT for 4 days in the LIT.

Assuming no more "events" like whatever happened in week 2, the outcome in week 4 would be exactly the same as the outcome in week 3. As a matter of fact as long as we outlaw labor and credit markets, the outcome in week 3 would repeat itself every week after week 3 forever.[18] The 990 would continue to work 5 days, consume 2 bushels of corn, and accumulate no additional corn every week. While it would clearly be to their advantage to work on Saturday or Sunday to accumulate more seed corn, and be able to work longer in the CIT and less in the LIT in subsequent weeks, the societal ban on weekend labor prevents them from doing this. The 10 who for some reason got one extra bushel of corn during week 2 will continue to work 2 days in the CIT, consume 2 bushels of corn, and accumulate no more seed corn beyond the 2 bushels they replace each week. At first this may seem strange because having more seed corn is clearly advantageous, so why would these 10 people stop after working two days in the CIT? Why would they not go ahead and work

---

[18] "Forever" is not hyperbole here because, as we are about to see, under the rules of autarky nobody would accumulate more seed corn, the stock, or supply of seed corn in the economy would not increase from week to week, and therefore seed corn would remain scarce forever. As we will see at some point this would cease to be the case once there is a labor or credit market.

on Wednesday, Thursday, or Friday in the LIT to accumulate more corn and be able to work less in subsequent weeks? The reason is there is no incentive for them to do so because no matter how much seed corn they may have at the beginning of any week, they would still have to work 2 days in the CIT if they must replace any seed corn they use. As long as there is no labor market -- where they could use their additional seed corn to hire others and put them to work in the CIT for a profit – and no credit market – where they could lend their additional seed corn and receive interest -- there is no incentive for the 10 to work more than 2 days in any week, and like the 990 they will just keep doing what they did in week 3 forever. To summarize: As long as labor and credit markets are banned, i.e. under the "rules" of *autarky*, inequality in outcomes is the same every week starting in week 3: 990 people work 5 days while 10 people work only 2 days, a difference of 3 days. Because nobody will accumulate more seed corn, the aggregate supply of seed corn will not increase after week 3, seed corn will remain scarce forever, and outcomes will be the same every subsequent week as in week 3.

This concludes our analysis of what will happen as long as there are no further "events" such as whatever took place in week 2, and as long as people are not permitted to enter into any economic relationships with one another. However, while inequality each week is the same, 3 days, obviously as the weeks go by *cumulative inequality grows arithmetically*, by 3 days every week, forever. We summarize these results for 8 weeks in table 1.

Table 1: Efficiency, Corn Stock, and Inequality under Autarky[19]

WK	Eff	CornStock	Days	DaysCum	Corn	CornCum
1	.40000	1000	0	0	0	0
2	.40200	1010	0	0	1	1
3	.40241	1010	3	3	0	1
4	.40241	1010	3	6	0	1
5	.40241	1010	3	9	0	1
6	.40241	1010	3	12	0	1
7	.40241	1010	3	15	0	1
8	.40241	1010	3	18	0	1

---

[19] The CornStock column gives the stock of seed corn in the economy at the *end* of each week.

What does the data in table 1 tell us about the effect of private ownership of scarce, non-labor, productive assets – in our case seed corn -- on outcomes?

- Having more of a non-labor productive asset makes people more productive.[20]

- If people own different amounts of a non-labor productive asset outcomes will be unequal.[21]

- The two conclusions above are true if, but only if, the non-labor asset is scarce, and therefore having more of it would, in fact, make people more productive.[22]

Table 1 also tells us that whatever occurred during week 2 to cause 10 people to each end up with an extra unit of seed corn enables each of them to work 18 fewer days than everyone else by the end of week 8. Is it possible that whatever those 10 people did differently than the other 990 people in week 2 *deserves* this much more compensation? Perhaps. But if so, we would then have to ask if it merits as many as 36 days off -- because by the end of week 14 that is what their compensation will have risen to.

In sum: *Under autarky the moral "dilemma" is that compensation for something that occurred in a single week rises* **arithmetically***, and does so* **forever***, since under the rules of autarky seed corn will remain scarce forever.*

---

[20] In our model the first bushel of seed corn will increase a person's productivity, as will the second, while a third will make no difference since 2 bushels allows a person to work entirely in the CIT.

[21] In our model, under the rules of autarky owning more than 2 bushels is of no use to anyone, so if anyone owns more than 2 bushels we should convert that to 2 bushels before calculating whether some own more than others.

[22] In our model seed corn is scarce for individuals as long as they have fewer than 2 bushels, and scarce for the economy as long as there is not enough so all production could take place in the CIT.

To see what role labor and credit markets play, and what happens when accumulation reaches the point where a productive asset ceases to be scarce, we must change the rules in our economy. Suppose we do this before week 4 begins, and announce that people are now free to hire others to work for them as their employees, or hire themselves out to work for others as they please. In other words, suppose we open a "free" labor market in week 4. Are there daily wage rates at which some would be willing to be employers and others willing to be employees? Is there an equilibrium wage rate we would expect to prevail in our simple economy?

Suppose the wage rate were lower than ¼ bushel per day. Nobody would be willing to work as an employee because anyone can get ¼ bushel a day working for herself in the LIT. Suppose the wage rate were higher than 1 bushel per day. In this case nobody would be willing to be an employer. If they put their employee to work in the LIT for a day they would only produce ¼ bushel of corn, which is less than their wage, which makes profits negative. If they put their employee to work with 1 bushel of seed corn for a day in the CIT their employee would produce 2 bushels on Sunday, but 1 bushel would go to replace the bushel used up, and after paying more than 1 bushel in wages, again profits would be negative. So we have discovered that the *feasible range* of daily wage rates in our labor market is ¼ ≤ w ≤ 1 bushels, because if w < ¼ bushel per day there will be nobody willing to be an employee, whereas if w > 1 bushel per day there will be nobody willing to be an employer.

While different employers and employees may start to strike deals at different wage rates in the feasible range on Monday morning, the *laws of supply and demand* tell us to expect two things to happen. First, there will be a tendency for the range of wage rates at which deals are struck to narrow. If employees are being hired by employers at a higher wage rate in one part of the labor market than another, there is an incentive for employees to flock to where the wage rate is higher, driving down the wage rate there. And there is an incentive for employers to flock to where the wage rate is lower, driving up the wage rate there. Presumably if people are free to seek employment and employees wherever they choose, any discrepancies in wage rates will be whittled away, and all deals will eventually be struck at nearly the same daily wage rate. However, this does not tell us what this single wage rate will be.

Suppose w = ½ bushel of corn per day. Each of the 990 people with 1 bushel of seed corn will first work in the CIT with their own bushel, which nets them 1 bushel for consumption after replacing the bushel they use up. After which they will apply to work as someone else's employee for ½ bushel per day for 2 days to get the other bushel they need for consumption -- since that is a better option than working for themselves in the LIT for only ¼ bushel per day. When 990 people are each looking for 2 days of work as someone else's employee, this generates a *supply of 1880 days of labor* in the labor market.

What is the best any of the 10 people who start week 4 with 2 bushels of seed corn can do? If they hire 2 days of labor to work with their 2 bushels in the CIT to produce 4 bushels of corn, they would end up with 1 bushel in profits after replacing the 2 bushels used up and paying 2 days times ½ bushel per day = 1 bushel in wages. To get the other 1 bushel they need to consume they would have to work 4 days in the LIT. If they use 1 bushel to work 1 day in the CIT themselves, and use 1 bushel to hire an employee to work 1 day in the CIT, of the 4 bushels produced 2 would be needed for replacement, ½ bushel would be paid in wages, leaving 1 and ½ bushels for consumption, and they would have to work 2 days in the LIT to get the other ½ bushel they need. In which case they would have to work 1 day in the CIT and 2 days in the LIT, or 3 days in total. On the other hand if they simply work themselves with their 2 bushels of seed corn 2 days in the CIT they will have 2 bushels after replacement for consumption. So if w = ½ bushel per day, the 10 people who start week 4 with 2 bushels will work with their 2 bushels of seed corn themselves in the CIT, not offer to hire anyone, and *the demand for labor will be zero*. Clearly, at w = ½ bushel per day, there will be excess supply in the labor market, and consequently the wage rate will be bid down below ½ bushel per day.

Readers can verify that if the wage rate were one third bushel per day there will still be excess supply of labor. As a matter of fact, there will continue to be excess supply of labor until the wage rate is bid down to w = ¼ bushel per day, the lower extreme of the feasible range for the wage rate. Only when w reaches ¼ bushel per day, the *equilibrium wage rate* in our simple economy's labor market, is there no longer excess supply, and further pressure driving the wage rate down.

Now that we know that if we open a labor market and allow the laws of supply and demand to operate the equilibrium wage rate will be ¼ bushel per day, we are ready to see what people in our economy will choose to do in week 4. Recall that 990 people begin week 4 with 1 bushel of seed corn, while 10 people begin week 4 with 2 bushels of seed corn.

Each of the 990 can do the best for themselves by working 1 day in the CIT with their own bushel of corn to get 1 bushel for consumption after replacement, and then work 4 more days whether it be for themselves in the LIT, for someone else as an employee, or some combination of the two -- since no matter how they work those additional 4 days they can only get ¼ bushel per day. So each of these 990 will work a total of 5 days.

No matter what the 10 choose to do they will have to work 2 days in week 4 to get 2 bushels for consumption. If they use their 2 bushels of corn to hire 2 days of labor and put them to work in the CIT, their employees will produce 4 bushels of corn. After replacing the 2 bushels used up, and paying their employees 2 days times ¼ bushel per day = ½ bushel in wages, they will have 1 and ½ bushels in profit left over. At which point they will have to work 2 days themselves in the LIT in order to get the other ½ bushel they need for consumption. Or, they could work with 1 bushel themselves in the CIT, and use 1 bushel to hire 1 day of labor. But that would leave them with only 1 and ¾ bushels, and they would have to work 1 day in the LIT to get the other ¼ bushel they need for consumption. Or, they could just use their 2 bushels to work 2 days in the CIT themselves, and end up with 2 bushels to consume. In short, no matter what the 10 who begin week 4 with 2 bushels of corn choose to do, they will have to work 2 days themselves to get their 2 bushels of corn to consume.

However, unlike under the rules of autarky where the 10 had no incentive to ever begin a week with more than 2 bushels of seed corn, now these 10 people have an incentive to accumulate more seed corn, because now they can use it to hire employees, earn more profits, and work less than 2 days themselves in future weeks.

How much seed corn would someone have to have at the beginning of a week in order not to have to work at all? Call this amount X. Then X times ¾ bushels in profits per bushel must equal the 2 bushels needed for consumption: $(3/4) X = 2$ bushels, and therefore $X = 8/3 = 2.6667$ bushels. So anyone who begins a week with 2.6667 bushels of seed corn has enough seed corn so when they hire 2.6667 days of labor at $w = ¼$ bushel per day, they will receive 2 bushels of corn in profits for consumption without doing any work themselves. And since they always replace any seed corn used up in the CIT, they can do this for every week forever once they have 2.6667 bushels at the beginning of some week. Moreover, anyone who has *more* than 2.6667 bushels of seed corn to start a week will never have to work again, *and* will be able to accumulate amounts of corn every week which will increase exponentially. Whereas there was no incentive for the 10 to work more than 2 days in week 3, under autarky now, after we open a labor market in week 4, clearly there is.[23]

If the 10 work a third day in the LIT in week 4 they can accumulate ¼ bushel more to start week 5. If they work a fourth day in the LIT they can accumulate ½ bushel more. And if they work a fifth day in the LIT in week 4 they will accumulate $¾ = .7500$ bushels more. So, after working 2 days in the CIT with their 2 bushels of seed corn, by working three additional days in the LIT in week 4 these 10 people can accumulate enough seed corn to start week 5 with 2.7500 bushels of seed corn, which is slightly more than 2.6667 units. In which case none of the 10 will ever have to work again, *and*, as we will see, their stocks of corn will now begin to grow exponentially -- all while the 990 continue to work 5 days a week forever with stocks of corn that remain at one.

Strictly speaking, given the assumptions we stipulated about people's preferences, there would be no reason for any of the 10 people to work enough in week 4 to begin week 5 with any more than 2.6667 bushels. Once they have 2.6667 bushels they will always be able to consume 2 bushels a week and they will never have to work again. Under our assumptions about their preferences, once they are able to consume 2 bushels and work no days every week, they have literally "maxed out." And

---

[23] There is also an incentive for the 990 to work more in order to accumulate more seed corn. However, they are working 5 days already, so unlike the 10 who are only working 2 days, they cannot work more to accumulate more.

since it takes a little extra work in week 4 to start week 5 with 2.7500 bushels instead of 2.6667, and we have assumed that people dislike work, they might not do it. However, in this case accumulation of seed corn would stop after week 4, seed corn would never cease to be scarce, and we would not be able to examine the effects of accumulation on scarcity and outcomes.

Week 4: So in the interest of generating "data" that permit consideration of this important issue, we assume the 10 people place some value on accumulating ever greater stocks of seed corn sufficient to induce them to work 3 extra days in week 4, to begin week 5 with 2.7500 bushels of seed corn. In which case in week 4 we have:

Efficiency is: 2000 bushels of corn for consumption + 10(.7500) = 7.5 bushels for accumulation = 2007.5 bushels of net corn produced, divided by (5)(990)+(5)(10) = 5000 days worked: 2007.5/5000 = .40150.
Work inequality is: 5 days – 5 days = 0 days.
Accumulation inequality is: .75 bushels – 0 bushels = .75 bushels.

Week 5: In week 5 the 990 would continue to work 5 days, replace all their seed corn, consume 2 bushels of corn, and accumulate nothing. While the incentive for them to accumulate more seed corn now that there is a labor market is even greater than before, they cannot because they are already working 5 days and cannot work on Saturday or Sunday. But 10 people who responded to the new opportunity introduced by the labor market to work 5 days instead of 2 in week 4 in order to accumulate an extra .7500 units of corn, have 2.7500 units of seed corn to use to hire employees in week 5. At $w = \frac{1}{4}$ bushels per day, and profits at $\frac{3}{4}$ bushels per day, they will collect (2.7500)(.75) = 2.0625 bushels of corn in profits, consume 2 bushels, and have .0625 bushels left over to add to their stock of seed corn without having worked at all.[24]

Efficiency is: 2000 bushels of corn for consumption + 10(.0625) = .625

---

[24] At this point since the 10 no longer have to work at all, they would be willing to hire employees for a wage rate higher than ¼ bushel per day. However, as long as seed corn remains scarce, the laws of supply and demand will drive the wage rate down to ¼ bushel per day so they won't have to pay more.

bushels for accumulation = 2000.625 bushels of net corn produced, divided by (5)(990)+(0)(10) = 4950 days worked: 2000.625/4950 = .40417.
Work inequality is: 5 days – 0 days = 5 days.
Accumulation inequality is: .0625 bushels – 0 bushels = .0625 bushels.

Week 6: While 990 continue to work 5 days, consume 2 bushels of corn, and accumulate no corn, the 10 would have 2.7500 + .0625 = 2.8125 units of corn to use to hire employees. At ¾ bushels in profits per day hired they would get 2.1094 bushels of corn in profits, consume 2 bushels, and have .1094 bushels to add to their stock, without having to work at all.

Efficiency is: 2000 bushels of corn for consumption + 10(.1094) = 1.094 bushels for accumulation = 2001.094 bushels of net corn produced, divided by (5)(990)+(0)(10) = 4950 days worked: 2001.094/4950 = .40426.
Work inequality is: 5 days – 0 days = 5 days.
Accumulation inequality is: .1094 bushels – 0 bushels = .1094 bushels.

Week 7: While the 990 continue to work 5 days, consume 2 bushels of corn, and accumulate no corn, the 10 would have 2.8125 + .1094 = 2.9219 bushels of corn to use to hire employees. At ¾ bushels in profits per day hired they would get 2.1914 bushels of corn in profits, consume 2 bushels, and have .1914 bushels to add to their capital stock without having to work.

Efficiency is: 2000 bushels of corn for consumption + 10(.1914) = 1.914 bushels for accumulation = 2001.914 bushels of net corn produced, divided by (5)(990)+(0)(10) = 4950 days worked: 2001.914/4950 = .40443.
Work inequality is: 5 days – 0 days = 5 days.
Accumulation inequality is: .1914 bushels – 0 bushels = .1914 bushels.

Week 8: While the 990 continue to work 5 days, consume 2 bushels of corn, and accumulate no corn, the 10 would have 2.9219 + .1914 = 3.1133 bushels of corn to use to hire employees. At ¾ bushels in profits per day hired they would get 2.3350 bushels of corn in profits, consume 2 bushels, and have .3350 bushels to add to their capital stock without having to work.

Efficiency is: 2000 bushels of corn for consumption + 10(.3350) = 3.350 bushels for accumulation = 2003.350 bushels of net corn produced,

divided by (5)(990)+(0)(10) = 4950 days worked: 2003.350/4950 = .40472.
Work inequality is: 5 days – 0 days = 5 days.
Accumulation inequality is: .3350 bushels – 0 bushels = .3350 bushels.

In sum, starting in week 5 we have a permanent inequality in days worked every week: 990 people work 5 days every week, while 10 people do no work after week 4. But in addition, inequality in corn stocks begins to escalate exponentially: 990 people maintain their corn stock at 1 unit from week 5 on, while 10 people increase their corn stock from 2.7500 bushels at the beginning of week 5, to 2.8125 bushels at the beginning of week 6, to 2.9219 bushels at the beginning of week 7, to 3.1133 bushels at the beginning of week 8, etc.

What if beginning in week 4 we legalize a credit market instead of a labor market? *While this may come as a surprise, the results will be exactly the same as those summarized in table 2.* [25] The equilibrium rate of interest will be r = ¾ bushels per week. The opportunity to lend seed corn at a positive rate of interest will induce each of the 10 to work 3 extra days in the LIT in week 4 to accumulate an extra .7500 bushels of seed corn to begin week 5 with 2.7500 bushels. While the 990 have the same incentive to accumulate, since they are already working 5 days in week 4 they will be unable to benefit from the credit market, just as they were unable to benefit from the labor market.

In week 5 each of the 10 will loan their 2.7500 bushels to some of the 990 at an interest rate of r = ¾ bushels per week, giving them (.75)(2.7500) = 2.0625 bushels of corn in interest.. After consuming 2 bushels this will allow each of the 10 to add .0625 bushels to their seed stock, and therefore be able to lend 2.7500 + .0625 = 2.8125 bushels in week 6. Obviously outcomes in weeks 7 and 8 will also be exactly the same as when we open a labor market. As long as seed corn remains scarce -- so the laws of supply and demand in the credit market drive the interest rate up to the upper end

---

[25] Those interested can analyze the workings of the credit market in our simple economy just as we analyzed the labor market above. Arbitrage will reduce discrepancies between interest rates contracted by different borrowers and lenders. Since nobody will lend at an interest rate lower than zero bushels per week, and nobody will borrow for an interest rate higher than ¾ bushels per week, the feasible range of interest rates will be $0 \leq r \leq 3/4$ bushels per week. And as long as seed corn is scarce the laws of supply and demand will drive the interest rate up to the upper extreme in the feasible range, r = ¾ bushels per week.

of its feasible range -- the 990 will continue to have to work 5 days every week, whether or not they participate in the credit market. In short, the results in table 2 below are exactly the same whether we open a labor or a credit market in week 4.[26]

Table 2: Efficiency, Aggregate Corn Stocks, and Inequality when a Labor or Credit Market Opens in Week 4

WK	Eff	CornStock	Days	DaysCum	Corn	CornCum
1	.40000	1000.000	0	0	0	0
2	.40200	1010.000	0	0	1	1
3	.40241	1010.000	3	3	0	1
4	.40150	1017.500	0	3	.7500	1.7500
5	.40417	1018.125	5	8	.0625	1.8125
6	.40426	1019.219	5	13	.1094	1.9219
7	.40443	1021.133	5	18	.1914	2.1133
8	.40472	1024.483	5	23	.3350	2.4483

How does a labor or credit market change outcomes?

- A labor or credit market increases incentives for those with more seed corn to accumulate more seed corn than they have an incentive to do under autarky.

- The additional seed corn they accumulate further increases economic efficiency by putting more people to work in the CIT as employees or borrowers.

---

[26] The reason we get exactly the same results from a credit market as from a labor market is that our simple model abstracts from a number of real world conditions -- increasing returns to scale and uncertainty to name two. However, this model nicely captures important similarities between labor and credit markets as economic "institutions," both of which permit *some* to benefit from increases in the productivity of the labor of *others*.

- As long as seed corn remains scarce the efficiency gain from additional accumulation is captured entirely by employers or lenders, which aggravates inequality.[27]

- If neither the supply of labor nor productive technologies change, eventually the 10 who get more seed corn in week 2 will accumulate enough seed corn to render seed corn abundant.

- Once seed corn is no longer scarce, i.e. once there are enough bushels at the beginning of a week so all corn can be produced in the CIT, the demand for labor will exceed the supply at any wage rate below 1 bushel per day, offers to lend seed corn will exceed the demand to borrow seed corn at any rate of interest higher than zero, and consequently everyone will have to work 2 days per week from that point on.

Table 2 demonstrates that by the end of week 8 -- only six weeks after whatever took place in week 2 -- 10 people will each have worked 23 fewer days than the other 990 people, *and* each of those same 10 people will have accumulated 2.4483 more bushels of corn than each of the other 990 people. Meanwhile the aggregate stock of seed corn in the economy has grown only from 1000 bushels at the beginning of week 1 to 1024.483 bushels at the end of week 8 and will remain scarce for quite some time.[28]

In sum: *When there is a credit or labor market the "dilemma" is that compensation for something which occurred in a single week rises* **exponentially***, and even though*

---

[27] Even if there were more technologies so capital could be substituted for labor incrementally, as long as capital remains scarce employers and lenders would still capture the lion's share of the efficiency gain.

[28] Until such time as all the corn we produce in a week can be produced in the CIT corn will remain scarce, and the daily wage rate remain at the low end of the feasible range, $w = \frac{1}{4}$ bushel per day. Or, alternatively, the weekly rate of interest will remain at the high end of the feasible range, $r = \frac{3}{4}$ bushels per week. We know that even if we produce no corn for accumulation we must produce at least 2000 bushels a week in order for each of the 1000 people to consume 2 bushels. To produce 2000 bushels in a week entirely in the CIT would require an aggregate stock of seed corn at the beginning of the week of 2000 bushels, which is still much greater than the 1024.483 bushels we have by the end of week 8.

compensation would cease when accumulation eventually renders seed corn abundant, this can easily occur long after cumulative compensation has become excessive.

The Philosophical Debate

The criticism of capitalist profits as immoral implicit in the "fundamental Sraffian theorem" begs the question of whether or not capitalists do something to deserve compensation even though they do no work, and produce no goods themselves. What happened in week 2 in our simple corn model that allowed 10 people to end up with one more bushel of corn than the other 990, and therefore be able to become capitalists and receive profit income in subsequent weeks? Did those 10 people do something for which they *deserve* to be compensated later on?

If extra seed corn is acquired through an illegal or immoral act, then presumably any future "fruits" of such an act are morally tainted as well. According to the "fruit of a poisonous tree legal doctrine" if evidence of guilt is obtained illegally it cannot generally be used to convict. But what if it is not the case that 10 people robbed or tricked the other 990 people into giving them a bushel of corn in week 2? What if, for example, it rained more heavily on the fields where 10 people worked in week 2 than on the fields where the other 990 worked? Some argue that because the 10 people who harvest an extra bushel of corn because it rained more where they worked committed no immoral act, therefore it is not unfair that they have an extra bushel at the end of week 2. Others argue that these 10 did nothing to deserve their good luck, and more to the point, the 990 people who worked where less rain happened to fall did nothing to deserve their bad luck.

What if 10 people each inherit an extra bushel of corn in week 2 while 990 people do not? Some argue that the heirs did not act immorally, and whoever made the bequests should be free to dispose of their wealth as they choose. Others argue that those who inherited the corn did nothing to deserve their inheritance, and more to the point, the 990 who inherited nothing do not deserve to be disadvantaged.[29]

---

[29] If the 10 bushels inherited were not produced in week 2 then our calculations of how efficient the economy was in week 2 need to be revised. But more importantly,

What if in week 2 when 10 people work 5 days just like everyone else, consume 2 bushels just like everyone else, and work no harder than anyone else, they each produce an extra unit of corn because they are more productive workers? Many argue that those who are more productive deserve greater compensation. While others argue that if the less productive are so *through no fault of their own*, it is *unfair* when the more productive enjoy greater economic benefits than the less productive.

What if 10 people work more days in week 2 to get their extra bushel of corn? Because we stipulated that working on Saturday or Sunday is illegal it is impossible for anyone to work more days since everyone is already working five days. However, we can easily tweak this rule to allow people to work extra days. We can go back to a time when Saturday was a legal work day, and ask what the moral implications are if 10 people work enough Saturdays[30] to accumulate an extra bushel of seed corn at the beginning of some week, while the other 990 people continue to enjoy two day weekends. Surely these industrious people deserve compensation because they work more days than others who chose to enjoy more leisure.

Or, we could tweak the rule that everyone must consume 2 bushels of corn every week. In which case, what if 10 people tighten their belts in week 2 and consume only 1 bushel of corn, in order to begin week 3 with an additional unit of seed corn, while 990 people continue to eat two bushels per week? Surely those who now have an extra unit of seed corn to begin week 3 deserve compensation for their "abstinence."

---

the debate over the morality of inheritance is legendary. I refer readers to chapter 1, "Economic Justice," in Robin Hahnel, *Economic Justice and Democracy: from competition to cooperation* (New York NY: Routledge, 2005) for my *rebuttal* to what I consider to be the strongest moral defense of inheritance: Namely, that even if those who inherit wealth may not deserve it, outlawing inheritance is an unfair infringement on the freedom to those who wish to bequeath wealth they may have acquired fairly.

[30] They would not need to work 4 full Saturdays to get an extra unit of seed corn because after the first Saturday they would have an extra ¼ bushel to work with in the CIT where they are more productive, etc.

Finally, what if 10 people simply work harder, and by making the sacrifice of exerting greater effort, increase the amount of corn they produce? If 10 people increase their effort and produce an extra unit of corn in week 2, while 990 choose not to, surely those who work harder deserve compensation.

Ultimately, the philosophical debate over the moral standing of what causes some people to have more seed corn than others at the end of week 2 must be engaged. And no doubt there will continue to be disagreements. However, as we have already seen from the data in tables 1 and 2 important moral dilemmas arise *irrespective* of where one comes down in this philosophical debate. Suppose one believes the 10 people who end up with an extra bushel of corn at the close of week 2 came by it fair and square and deserve compensation. How large should the compensation be? Doesn't size matter?

The Moral Dilemma that Cannot be Escaped

Suppose we have decided that compensation is deserved. When is it too little?... Too much?... Or, as Goldilocks famously said: Just right? The easiest way to see that there is no avoiding a serious moral dilemma whenever productive assets are owned privately is to consider the case where people earn a moral right to compensation by working more days. We can simplify calculations by assuming that people are immortal, don't care when they work, and people who work more days in one week are compensated by awarding them days off in subsequent weeks.

In this case it is reasonable to conclude that anyone who works 4 more days than others in the LIT in early weeks to accumulate an extra bushel of seed corn to start some week with 2 bushels instead of 1, deserves 4 days off in later weeks as compensation. Under these assumptions 4 days off is compensation that is *commensurate* with the 4 extra days these people worked which others did not. However, under the rules of autarky anyone with 2 bushels of seed corn need only work 2 days a week, while others with only 1 bushel must work 5 days a week – compensation of 3 days off per week. Which means that compensation *commensurate* with sacrifice – 4 days off -- will have occurred before the second week is over -- *yet compensation will continue to rise arithmetically forever.*

As table 2 makes clear, if there is a labor or credit market, not only will compensation soon rise to 5, not 3 fewer days worked per week, those who work 5 fewer days will begin to accumulate ever more corn than others as well. Total cumulative compensation will soon exceed four days off, *yet compensation will continue to rise exponentially until seed corn is no longer scarce.*

In sum, even if those who initially come to have more seed corn do so in a manner which deserves compensation:

- If corn can be privately owned, even if people enter into no economic relations whatsoever, accumulation will cease before seed corn becomes abundant, and cumulative compensation will eventually exceed the amount which can be morally justified.

- If seed corn can be privately owned *and* people are "free" to enter into employment and credit relations, over compensation will be even more excessive, although in theory accumulation might eventually render seed corn abundant, at which point the advantage of owning more seed corn would cease.

The Most Difficult Moral Case

When we make it legal to work on Saturdays, why do 10 people take advantage of the opportunity while 990 people do not? Immortals with a zero rate of time discount should not care when they work, so trading more days off later for fewer days worked earlier is clearly the rational strategy, and everyone should do it. We can strengthen the argument that the 990 deserve what they get by stipulating that all are equally able to work on Saturdays – there are no single mom's without childcare available on weekends. We can further stipulate that the industrious share their wisdom and enlighten their less wise comrades about the advantages of working more days in early weeks -- but to no avail. What are the wise supposed to do if they cannot enlighten their comrades? Are the industrious morally compelled not to work more in early weeks if they cannot convince others to do likewise?

Even if we apply the distributive maxim *compensation commensurate with sacrifice* strictly, this does not require foregoing the efficiency gain from some who are wise working more in early weeks. It simply requires sharing the benefit of that efficiency gain equitably. What the maxim requires in this, admittedly, *most difficult moral case* is:

- First, compensate the industrious who work 4 more days than others in early weeks *fully* for their extra sacrifice by allowing them to take 4 days off later whenever they want to.

- After which, distributive justice requires that everyone must work the same number of days. But notice that since the extra sacrifice of the industrious increases the stock of seed corn in the economy, which increases labor productivity in the economy, *everyone* will be able to work fewer days than before.

Does strict application of the distributive maxim *compensation commensurate with sacrifice* penalize the wise and industrious? Some argue that it does *not* because we have fully compensated the industrious for their extra days of work in early weeks with an equal number of days off later, *and* the wise benefit from their industry equally with the less wise as all now work less than before. Others point out that the 990 who did not work more in early weeks -- even though their wiser comrades explained to them why it would be to their advantage to do so -- have benefited just as much as the industrious.

As you might have expected, because distributive justice is ultimately a philosophical question, about which people often have a personal interest, conclusions are more widely disputed than in other areas of economics. Which is not to say that economic models such as the one used here do not shed light on where the important issues in debates over distributive justice lie.

CONCLUSION: WHAT LIES AHEAD?

There is some very bad news that over shadows everything else: We are currently on pace to trigger cataclysmic climate change in only a few decades, and so far seem unable to take necessary counter measures. We have exhausted the sink capacity of the upper atmosphere to store greenhouse gas emissions from the fossil fuels we burn when producing goods and services. If we do not reduce global carbon emissions dramatically in the next few decades, and reach zero net emissions by midcentury, we will change climate conditions in highly undesirable ways at a minimum, and risk triggering cataclysmic climate change of Biblical proportions.[31]

The core dilemma that humanity has failed to overcome is what economists call the *free rider problem*: When anyone goes to the trouble and expense to reduce carbon emissions others benefit as much as they do. Which means there is an incentive for everyone not to reduce emissions themselves, but instead try to wait and "free ride" on the emission reductions of others. It is also clear that current levels of other environmental throughputs are unsustainable, and if not reduced will soon damage several other important ecosystems beyond repair.

The second piece of bad news is that economic inequality has increased faster over the past half century than at any time for which we have credible data, and escalating inequality shows no sign of abating. Moreover, a strong case can be made that most of the recent increase in economic inequality is *not* morally justifiable. The only silver lining in this regard is that economic growth in a few large, poor countries has recently outstripped economic growth in richer countries, slightly dampening the rise of global income inequality.

A third piece of economic bad news is that many economists and most governments have *un*learned the lessons Keynes taught us during the Great Depression, namely:

- Absent prudent financial regulation the financial sector is an accident waiting to happen, and destined to trigger new financial crises which lead in turn to economic recessions, or worse.

---

[31] The most recent United Nations climate report https://www.ipcc.ch/sr15/ is a *must read* for *everyone*.

- Timely, adequate, fiscal stimulus and/or expansionary monetary policy should be applied to avoid huge, wasteful losses in production as workers and factories sit idle during economic recessions or depressions.

The most important change in the history of capitalism was triggered when things went so haywire after the Crash of 1929 and the Great Depression that followed, that economists and politicians were compelled to take Keynes' advice and finally embrace financial regulation and macroeconomic stabilization policies. But soon after Richard Nixon opined in 1971 that "we are all Keynesians now," Keynesian wisdom was unlearned by many in the economics profession and by mainstream politicians alike.

The most egregious recent example of government failure to respond effectively to curtail a recession because it focused instead on limiting government budget deficits, is the European Union, where double digit unemployment rates were tolerated for ten years after the Great Recession struck in 2008. While less guilty, the Obama administration in the United States deferred far too much to *deficit hawks,* and administered a fiscal stimulus in 2009 that was only half the size needed, unnecessarily prolonging recovery from the Great Recession in the US. On the other hand, the response to the financial crisis was somewhat stronger in Europe than in the US, where the Dodd-Frank Wall Street Reform and Consumer Protection Act passed in 2010 was woefully inadequate to begin with, and has been eroded further as compliant politicians in Washington continue to succumb to relentless pressure from the financial industry.

The good news on the economic front is that the human capacity to discover new, innovative products and technologies has never been greater. The expansion of access to information and communication for billions of people worldwide through the internet, satellites, smart phones, cyber-optic cable, and high speed computation is an immense technological achievement. Recent improvements in solar and wind technologies driving down the cost of producing renewable energy is no less astounding, as is the immense potential of artificial intelligence. And all-electric automobiles are already affordable, which means that only the replacement of gasoline station infrastructure with electric recharging stations stands in the way of electrifying automobile fleets.

How we will respond to the economic challenges that confront us in the decades ahead remains to be seen. Can we reform the current economic system fast enough and deeply enough to avoid environmental and/or social collapse? Will we eventually replace the current economic system with a system that distributes the burdens and benefits of economic activity fairly, is less prone to destroy the natural environment, and empowers workers to manage themselves? In short, will we continue to engage in the economics of competition and greed, or will we finally learn how to practice the economics of equitable cooperation?

The only prediction I feel it is safe to make is this: Francis Fukuyama was wrong when he famously predicted that we have seen the "end of history" -- that unlike all previous economic systems, *neoliberal capitalism* is here to stay indefinitely. Because I find it hard to believe we can continue on our present course, I expect the remainder of economic history in the twenty-first century to be full of economic twists and turns. Hopefully this short economic primer will help prepare its readers to both understand this history and affect it for the better as it unfolds.

ABOUT THE AUTHOR

Robin Hahnel is Professor Emeritus from the American University in Washington DC. He has also taught as a visiting professor at the University of Maryland, Lewis and Clark College, Portland State University, Willamette University, the Catholic University of Panama, the Catholic University of Peru, and the University of Manchester in England. He is author, or co-author, of fifteen books, fourteen book chapters, forty articles in refereed economic journals, and over a hundred articles in magazines and newspapers on different aspects of economic theory and policy. He resides in Portland, Oregon with his family.

www.ingramcontent.com/pod-product-compliance
Lightning Source LLC
Chambersburg PA
CBHW030017190526
45157CB00016B/3082